MULTIPLE CH QUESTIONS
IN
PHYSIOLOGY

Dr. (Mrs.) Rashmi A. Joshi
Lecturer
Department of Physiology
Homoeopathic Medical College
Satara 145003(MS)

and

Dr. (Mrs.) Manju Saraswat
Principal
Tuka Ram Kanya Mahavidyalaya
Aligarh (UP)

B. Jain Publishers (P) Ltd.
New Delhi

MULTIPLE CHOICE QUESTIONS IN PHYSIOLOGY

First Edition: 2002

Price: Rs. 90.00

Published by:
Kuldeep Jain
for
B. Jain Publishers (P) Ltd.
1921, Street No. 10, Chuna Mandi,
Paharganj, New Delhi 110 055 (INDIA)
Phones: 3670430; 3670572; 3683200, 3683300
Fax: 011-3610471 & 3683400
Email: bjain@vsnl.com
Website: www.bjainbooks.com

Printed in India by:
J.J. Offset Printers
7, Printing Press Area, Ring Road,
Wazirpur, Delhi - 110035

ISBN: 81-8056-210-7   **BOOK CODE: BJ-5672**

P R E F A C E

It is our pleasure and privilege to present the first edition of multiple choice questions in physiology.It is difficult to catch up with the enormously expanding field of Physiology.The students who are reviewing or studying physiology for medical examination ,B.Sc.,M.Sc. and other paramedical courses will find it useful.The questions are prepared to give best satisfaction to teachers and students. Endevour has been made to cover all the necessary aspects of physiology in touch with evolution, cell and genetics. This book offers over thousand questions (MCQs) incorporating the concepts and principles involved in physiology. The questions and answers have been prepared after consulting various standard textbooks of physiology. Finally, healthy criticisim, suggestions from students and faculty members, as well as ideas to improve the standard and usefulness of the book will be highly appreciated.

Rashmi A. Joshi
Manju Saraswat

CONTENTS

Chapter 1

EVOLUTION

1. **The man who first experimentally proved that life could only come out of life was**
   (a) Redi
   (b) Louis Pasteur
   (c) Schwann
   (d) Weisman.

2. **It was believed that mosquitoes and snails arose spontaneously (Abiogenesic) from decaying matter. This was first refuted by**
   (a) Redi
   (b) Louis Pasteur
   (c) Darwin
   (d) Schwann.

3. **It is supposed that earth appeared as a big globe of hot liquids and gases about**
   (a) 1000 million years ago
   (b) 2000 million years ago
   (c) 8000 million years ago
   (d) 4700 million years ago.

4. **The theory of germ plasm was put forward by**
   (a) Cuvier
   (b) Muller
   (c) Weisman
   (d) Darwin.

5. **The virus was first discovered in 1892 by**

    (a) Schblaiden

    (b) Louis pasteur

    (c) Leeunhock

    (d) Ivanovshy.

6. **That the primitive atmosphere was composed of H, CH_4, H_2O, and CN was hypothesised by**

    (a) Oparin

    (b) Miller

    (c) Cuvier

    (d) Redi.

7. **The particle which is composed of an outer protein coat and iner DNA molecule is called**

    (a) Protist

    (b) Bacteriophage

    (c) Microbe

    (d) Bacteria.

8. **Tobacoo Mosaic Virus was the first to be isolated and it was done in 1935 by**

    (a) Leeuwenhoik

    (b) W.M. stanley

    (c) K. E. van baes

    (d) Wolff.

9. **The living nature of the viruses can only be seen by their**

    (a) Organic nature

    (b) Disease containing nature

    (c) Duplicating ability

    (d) Structure and composition.

60. Which of the processes mirrors the evolutionary history of organisms

(a) Physiology

(b) Anatomical structures

(c) Embryonic development

(d) Fossil study.

61. If the system exchanges neither matter nor energy with its surroundings it is called as

(a) Open

(b) Closed

(c) Systematic

(d) None.

62. Organisms which can synthesize some or all of their monomeric subunits, metabolic intermediates and macromolecules from CO_2 and NH_3 are called as

(a) Heterotrophs

(b) Autotrophs

(c) Chemotrophs

(d) Anaerobes.

63. Which of the following destroys H_2O_2 in the cell

(a) Glyoxysomes

(b) Peroxisomes

(c) Lysosomes

(d) Nucleosomes.

64. Which of the cell organelles convert fats into carbohydrates

(a) Peroxysomes

(b) Nucleosomes

(c) Glyoxysomes

(d) Lysosomes.

65. Which of the following process occurs before cytokinesis in cells
(a) Nuclear division
(b) Vacuolar division
(c) Cell division
(d) None.

66. The internal membrane of the chloroplast form stacks of closed cisternae called as
(a) Chlorophyll
(b) Thylakoids
(c) Cristae
(d) Cistron.

67. Which of the following convert solar energy into chemical energy in the cell
(a) Mitochondria
(b) Chloroplast
(c) Nucleus
(d) Vacuoles.

68. The origin of mitochondria and chlorophyll is probably from
(a) Photosynthetic bacteria
(b) Endosymbiotic bacteria
(c) Eukaryotic bacteria
(d) Cell.

69. The viruses outside the host cell are non living particles and are called as
(a) Viriod
(b) Phages
(c) Bacteriophages
(d) Virions.

70. **Which of the following is the known cell**
   (a) Lecuoplast
   (b) Nucleoplasm
   (c) Mycoplasm
   (d) Bacteria.

Answer sheet is at the end of the book.

Chapter 2

CELL

1. **In electron microscope the source of light used is**
   (a) Ordinary daylight
   (b) UV light
   (c) Infra-red light
   (d) Beams of electrons.

2. **The physical basis of life is**
   (a) Cytoplasm
   (b) Protoplasm
   (c) Nucleoplasm
   (d) Endoplasm.

3. **The comman immediate source of energy in cellular activities is**
   (a) ATP
   (b) TPN
   (c) ADP
   (d) PGAL.

4. **Double helix DNA model was given by**
   (a) Fisher and Haldane
   (b) Watson and Crick
   (c) Lamarck and Darwin
   (d) Hugo de Veries.

5. **Ribosomes are the centers for**
   (a) Respiration
   (b) Photosynthesis
   (c) Protein synthesis
   (d) Fat synthesis.

6. **The cell theory states that**
   (a) All cells have nuclei
   (b) All cells are living
   (c) Cells reproduce by mitosis
   (d) Cells are the functional and structural units of plants and animals.

7. **The purines of DNA are represented by**
   (a) Uracil and Guanine
   (b) Guanine and Adenine
   (c) Adenine and Cytosine
   (d) None of the above.

8. **How many types of RNA are found in cell**
   (a) 2
   (b) 3
   (c) 5
   (d) 6

9. **The first person to see a cell under the microscope was**
   (a) M. J. Schleiden
   (b) Theodor Schwann
   (c) Antony Van Leuwenhock
   (d) Robert Hooke.

10. **Plant cells difer from animals cells in one of the following ways**
    (a) All plant cells possess chlorophyll
    (b) Plant cells are biggest

(c) Plant cells have a rigid cell wall

(d) Plant cells are not so specialized.

11. **Chromosomes are concerned with**

(a) Respiration

(b) Growth

(c) Hereditary characters

(d) Assimilation.

12. **The ATP is formed in**

(a) Ribosomes

(b) Golgi bodies

(c) Mitochondria

(d) None of the above.

13. **The essential genetic material is**

(a) DNA

(b) RNA

(c) Fats and proteins

(d) Proteins.

14. **Plasma membrane controls**

(a) Absorption of water

(b) Passage of water and solutes in and out of cell

(c) Passage of water and solutes into the cell

(d) Passage of water and solutes out of the cell.

15. **Which of the following are linked together in long chains to form purines**

(a) Purines

(b) Amino acids

(c) Pyrimidines

(d) Sugars.

16. The pentose sugar present in DNA is

(a) Ribose

(b) Deoxyribose

(c) Sucrose

(d) None of the above.

17. The function of amyloplast is to

(a) Absorb water

(b) Absorb light

(c) Store fats

(d) Store starch.

18. Which base in place of thymine is present in RNA

(a) Adenine

(b) Uracil

(c) Cytosine

(d) Guanine.

19. Within a cell, the site of aerobic respiration is

(a) Ribosomes

(b) Mitochondria

(c) Golgi body

(d) Endoplasmic reticulum.

20. Which of the following cell organelle is considered to be rich in hydrolytic enzymes

(a) Endoplasmic reticulum

(b) Lysosomes

(c) Golgi complex

(d) Mitochondria.

21. **The DNA molecule is composed of**

(a) Pentose sugar, phosphoric acid and pyrimidines

(b) Pentose sugar, phosphoric acid, pyrimidines and purines

(c) Pentose sugar, phosphoric acid and purines

(d) Pentose sugar and hexose sugar.

22. **The largest cell organelle in the cells are**

(a) Plastids

(b) Golgi bodies

(c) Mitochondria

(d) Chromosomes.

23. **A cystolith is a deposit of**

(a) Calcium oxalate

(b) Starch

(c) Calcium carbonate

(d) Silica.

24. **Raphides are needle like crystals of calcium oxalate which are especially common in**

(a) Asparagus

(b) Dahlia

(c) Balsam

(d) Rose.

25. **Chromosomes having equal or almost equal arms are known as**

(a) Metacenteric

(b) Acrocentric

(c) Concentric

(d) Telocentric.

26. **Oxysomes are found in the**
    (a) Chloroplast
    (b) Nucleus
    (c) Mitochondria
    (d) Ribosomes.

27. **Quantasome consist of**
    (a) 100 chlorophyll molecule
    (b) 130 chlorophyll molecule
    (c) 230 chlorophyll molecule
    (d) 500 chlorophyll molecule.

28. **Cell walls of adjacent cells are connected by**
    (a) Primary cell wall
    (b) Secondary cell wall
    (c) Middle lamella
    (d) Cellulose.

29. **Chlorophyll is found in**
    (a) Leucoplast
    (b) Grana of chloroplast
    (c) Stroma
    (d) Membrane.

30. **Dictyosomes were discovered by**
    (a) J.Bonner
    (b) De Veries
    (c) C. Porter
    (d) C. Golgi.

31. **Xanthophyll is**
    (a) Colourless
    (b) Green Coloured
    (c) Yellow Coloured
    (d) Red Coloured.

32. **Centrosomes which are found in all animal cells, in plant cell these are**

   (a) Never found
   (b) Found in bryophytes
   (c) Occasionally found
   (d) Sometimes found in lower plants.

33. **The leucoplasts are**

   (a) Colourless
   (b) Coloured
   (c) Green
   (d) Red.

34. **The fluid part of a cell sap and it is the**

   (a) Non living content of cell
   (b) Living content of cell
   (c) Non living content of vacuole
   (d) Living content of vacuole.

35. **Basic structure of a nucleotide is composed of**

   (a) Phosphate-nitrogen
   (b) Phosphate-sugar-nitrogen
   (c) Protein-lipid
   (d) Phosphate-sugar.

36. **If one cell has tw]ice as much DNA as an ordinary cell, the probability is that the cell is**

   (a) Reproducing
   (b) Excreting
   (c) Respiring
   (d) Absorbing.

37. The term protoplasm was first given by
   a) Robert Hooke
   b) Robert Brown
   (c) Purkinje
   (d) Nirenberg.

38. The nucleus was first identified by
   (a) Singer
   (b) Altman
   (c) Robert Brown
   (d) Singleton.

39. The word endoplasmic reticulum was coined by
   (a) Altman
   (b) Watson and Crick
   (c) Porter and Kalmann
   (d) Muller.

40. Who discovered ribosomes in animal cells
   (a) Watson
   (b) Tatum
   (c) Cowdry
   (d) Palade

41. The word chromosome was first given by
   (a) Waldeyer
   (b) Robert Hooke
   (c) Hofmeister
   (d) Strassburger.

42. The formula of chlorophyll a is
   (a) $C_{55}H_{72}O_5N_4Mg$
   (b) $C_{55}H_{70}O_6N_4Fe$

(c) $C_{55}H_{70}O_5N_4Fe$

(d) $C_{55}H_{77}O_6N_4Mg$

43. The inner membrane of mitochondria is pushed in the form of plate like projections which are termed as

(a) Nuclei

(b) Cristae

(c) Lysosome

(d) Chromosome.

44. The oraganelle responsible for the formation of as in the cell divisions is

(a) Centrosome

(b) Ribosome

(c) Lysosome

(d) Chromosome.

45. What is the normal diameter of ribosome

(a) 5-30 μ

(b) 200-300Å

(c) 20-100Å

(d) 500Å.

46. The thickness of unit membrane is

(a) 75 Å

(b) 1 μ

(c) 5 - 30 μ

(d) 2 - 6 μ.

47. Central dogma of modern biology is

(a) DNA -> RNA -> PROTEIN

(b) RNA -> DNA -> protein

(c) RNA -> Protein -> DNA

(d) RNA -> Protein

48. An organelle which has electron transport system is

(a) Nucleus

(b) Centriole

(c) Ribosomes

(d) Mitochondria

49. The chemical substance abundantly present in middle lamella is

(a) Suberin

(b) Pectin

(c) Cutin

(d) Lignin.

50. The following sequence best arranges the compounds in order of increasing molecular weight

(a) tRNA- DNA- rRNA

(b) rRNA-DNA- tRNA

(c) DNA- tRNA- rRNA

(d) tRNA- rRNA- DNA

51. The maximum magnification possible with electron microscope is

(a) 200 times

(b) 2000 times

(c) 20.000 times

(d) 200,000 times.

52. The strongest evidence that DNA is a genetic material comes from

(a) Chromosomes

(b) Transformations of bacterial cells

(c) DNA is not present in cytoplasm

(d) DNA is present in nuclei.

53. Two strands of DNA are attached by hydrogen bonds between
   (a) A-T, G-C
   (b) A-C, G-T
   (c) A-G, T-C
   (d) A-U, G-C.

54. Peptide bonds are present in
   (a) Amino acids
   (b) Nucleic acids
   (c) Organic acids
   (d) Urea.

55. The process by which DNA molecule passes information to RNA is called as
   (a) Translocation
   (b) Transcription
   (c) Translation
   (d) Transduction.

56. Continuity of cytoplasm from cell to cell is maintained through
   (a) Nuclear pore
   (b) Middle lamella
   (c) Plasmodesmata
   (d) Pith.

57. Pigment anthocyanin is located in
   (a) Chromoplast
   (b) Chloroplast
   (c) Vacuole
   (d) Cytoplasm.

58. **A multinucleated cell is called as**

(a) Coenobium

(b) Thallus

(c) Synchytrium

(d) Coenocyte.

59. **Which of the following is an exception to cell theory**

(a) Fungi

(b) Viruses

(c) Bacteria

(d) Lichens.

60. **Lampbrush chromosomes are found in**

(a) Brain cells of cats

(b) Germ cells of mammlia

(c) Ovarina cells of amphibians

(d) Salivary glands of diptera.

61. **Basic structure of chromatin consists of**

(a) RNA wrapped around

(b) Non histone proteins wrapped around DNA

(c) DNA wrapped histones around

(d) Histone proteins wrapped around DNA.

62. **The cell organelle which shows extensive polymorphism is**

(a) Ribosome

(b) Lysosome

(c) Chloroplasts

(d) Dictyosome

63. Genome means

(a) Total number of genes present in a diploid cell

(b) Genotype of the organism

(c) Total number of chromosomes present in a gamete

(d) Total number of chromosomes present in an organism.

64. The chromosomal ends are known as

(a) Metamere

(b) Centromere

(c) Satellite

(d) Telomere.

65. Mitosis was discovered by

(a) Farmer and Moore

(b) Huxley

(c) Flemming

(d) None of the above.

66. Meiosis was first observed by

(a) Kostof

(b) Porter

(c) Farmer and Moore

(d) Kollikas.

67. The division of nucleus is known as

(a) Cytokinesis

(b) Karyokinesis

(c) Anaphase

(d) Karyophase.

68. The stage in which nuclear membrane and nucleolus disappear is known as

(a) Prophase

(b) Metaphase

(c) Anaphase

(d) Telophase

69. The chromosome can be best seen at

(a) Prophase

(b) Metaphase

(c) Anaphase

(d) Telophase

70. A metacenteric chromosome at metaphase stage will appear as

(a) I shaped

(b) J shaped

(c) L shaped

(d) V shaped.

71. In mitosis the centromere divides at

(a) Protoplast

(b) Metaphase

(c) Anaphase

(d) Telophase.

72. The chromosome is attached to spindle fiber by

(a) Satellite body

(b) Telomere

(c) Centromere

(d) Pellicle.

73. **The stage in which chromatids move towards the pole is known as**

   (a) Prophase

   (b) Metaphase

   (c) Anaphase

   (d) Telophase.

74. **In mitotic cell division the amount of DNA in daughter cell is**

   (a) Equal to parent cell

   (b) Half of the parent cell

   (c) Double of parent cell

   (d) None of the above.

75. **Meiosis and mitosis are unlike each other because in meiosis**

   (a) Homologous chromosomes pair and exhange parts

   (b) Chromosome number is valued

   (c) The four nuclei formed are not identical

   (d) All of the above.

Answer sheet is at the end of the book.

Chapter 3

HISTOLOGY

1. **The epidermis of the skin is derived from the germinal layer**
    (a) Mesoderm
    (b) Endoderm
    (c) Ectoderm
    (d) Neurectoderm.

2. **The layer of epidermis which is constantly replaced is**
    (a) Stratum compactum
    (b) Stratum malpghium
    (c) Stratum corneum
    (d) Stratum granulosum.

3. **The tough fibrous protein containing much sulphur which is secreted by the stratum corneum is**
    (a) Keratin
    (b) Carotene
    (c) Cornea
    (d) Chitin.

4. **The mesodermal derivative of the skin which is the dermis is a**
    (a) Glandular epithelium
    (b) Fibrous cartilage
    (c) Muscular tissue
    (d) Areolar tissue.

5.   **The type of protein in the dermis is**

   (a) Collagen
   (b) Keratin
   (c) Fibrin
   (d) Chitin.

6.   **The layer of cells that constantly replace the worn out cells is called**

   (a) Stratum corneum
   (b) Stratum malipighium
   (c) Startum compactum
   (d) Stratum granulosum.

7.   **The pigmentation of the skin found in the negroes and orientals is due to cells in dermils known as**

   (a) Melanophores
   (b) Lipophores
   (c) Granophores
   (d) Iridophores.

8.   **70% of body heat is lost through skin. The heat control is done by**

   (a) Corpucles of the skin
   (b) Dermis of skin
   (c) Hypothalamus
   (d) Medulla oblongata.

9.   **The function of the sweat glands is**

   (a) Removal of excess water
   (b) Removal of excess salts
   (c) Regulation of body temperature
   (d) Regulation of salt content.

10. **The tissue that helps in the conservation of heat is**
  (a) Vascular tissue
  (b) Glandular tissue
  (c) Aerolar tissue
  (d) Adipose tissue.

11. **In man, the sweat glands are not found in**
  (a) Pinna
  (b) Lips
  (c) Head
  (d) Nose.

12. **Claws, horns and hooves of mammals are derivatives of**
  (a) Stratum compactum
  (b) Stratum corneum
  (c) Unossified bone
  (d) Ossified cartilage.

13. **The hides of the cattle used in industries come from**
  (a) Skin
  (b) Dermis
  (c) Epidermis
  (d) Corneum.

14. **The 'gooseflesh' which is erection of hair on the skin is due to**
  (a) Stimulation of sympathetic system
  (b) Vasodilation of skin capillaries
  (c) Stimulation of parasympathetics
  (d) Stimulation of skin corpuscles.

15. **Arrector pillmuscle is found in dermis and it**
  (a) Contracts oil glands
  (b) Errects hair or fur
  (c) Causes vaso constriction
  (d) Moves the skin.

16. Skin glands are absent in animals such as
- (a) Elephants
- (b) Porpoises
- (c) Buffaloes
- (d) Bats.

17. The stratified epithelium is seen in
- (a) Capillaries
- (b) Veins
- (c) Buccal cavity
- (d) Muscles.

18. The endothelium of blood vessel is a type of
- (a) Squamous epithelium
- (b) Columnar epithelium
- (c) Ciliated epithelium
- (d) Glandular epithelium.

19. The basal granules are present at the base of
- (a) Cilia
- (b) Nucleus
- (c) Basement membrane
- (d) Plasma membrane.

20. The acini with regards to secretion are found in
- (a) Globlet cells
- (b) Ducts of glands
- (c) Multicellular glands
- (d) Unicellular glands.

21. In areolar connective tissue the yellow fibres are
- (a) Elastic and single
- (b) White and in bundles
- (c) Branched and nonelastic
- (d) Single and nonelastic

22. The gelatin is obtained when the connective tissue is boiled. It is obtained from

   (a) Fibres in the tissue

   (b) Yellow fibres

   (c) Collagen of matrix.

   (d) Elastin of fibres.

23. Most cells are connective tissue cells which may contain heparin or histamine and are found mostly in

   (a) Kidney tubes

   (b) Walls of blood vessels

   (c) Liver cells

   (d) Bone marrow.

24. Histiocyte is a connective tissue cell the funciton of which is

   (a) Phagocytic

   (b) Secretion

   (c) Sustenance

   (d) Fibre production.

25. Tendons of muscles and duramater of the brain are made up of

   (a) Areolar tissue

   (b) White fibrous tissue

   (c) Yellow fibrous tissue

   (d) Elastic tissue.

26. Yellow fibrous tissue is made up of

   (a) Periosteum

   (b) Ligaments

   (c) Perichondrium

   (d) Peritoneum.

27. In the bone the concentric rings around the Haversian canal which contain osteoblast are known as

(a) Matrix

(b) Lamellae

(c) Endosteum

(d) Periosteum.

28. The Volkmann's canals are transverse connections between

(a) Two haversian canals

(b) The lamellae

(c) Lamellae and Haversian

(d) Bone marrow and lamellae.

29. The Haversian canals contain

(a) Bone marrow

(b) Endosteum

(c) Artery and vein

(d) Collagen.

30. The bone marrow is largely made up of

(a) Connective tissue and bone

(b) Adipose tissue and blood vessels

(c) Blood vessels and nerves

(d) Endosteum and fibrous tissue.

31. The haemopoiesis or manufacture of erythrocytes and granulocytes occur in

(a) Yellow marrow

(b) Osbeoblasts

(c) Canaliculi

(d) Red marrow.

32. The type of cartilage that helps to avoid friction in ball and socket joints is
    (a) Myaline
    (b) Elastic
    (c) Fibrous
    (d) Calcified.

33. The intervertebral discs are made up of
    (a) Fibrous cartilage
    (b) Synovial membrane
    (c) Hyaline cartilage
    (d) Elastic fibres.

34. The striated muscle fibres are coenocytic which means that they are
    (a) Branched
    (b) Multinucleate
    (c) Uninucleate
    (d) In bundles.

35. The dark bonds or A-discs and light bands or J-discs are separated by 2 discs or
    (a) Sarcoplasm
    (b) Sarcolemma
    (c) Krauress membrane
    (d) Sarcostyles.

36. Bundles of striated muscles fiberes called fasciculi are enclosed by a sheath called
    (a) Epimysium
    (b) Endomysium
    (c) Perimysium
    (d) Peritoneum

37. The difference between the cardiac muscles and the striated voluntary muscles is that the former is

(a) Not coenoctic

(b) Hashicker J-discs

(c) Hashicker Z-discs

(d) Hashinner light bands.

38. The muscle that is never fatigued is

(a) Smooth muscle

(b) Cardiac muscle

(c) Sphincter muscle

(d) Vascular muscle.

39. The strongest muscles in man are the muscles of the

(a) Heart

(b) Biceps

(c) Thigh

(d) Jaws.

40. The cartilage forming the pinna is

(a) Elastic

(b) Hyaline

(c) Fibrous

(d) Calcified.

41. The red colour of the striated muscle fibre is due to

(a) Haemoglobin

(b) Capillaries

(c) Myohaemoglobin

(d) Oxyhaemoglobin.

42. The type of tissue found between muscles, mesenteries and between skin and body wall is

   (a) Tendon

   (b) Areolar

   (c) Epithelial

   (d) Membranous.

43. Matrix of bone contains a protein called ostein while the cartilage contains

   (a) Gelatin

   (b) Collagen

   (c) Chondrin

   (d) Myosin.

44. The muscle protein consists of a actomysin which breaks down to actin and myosin on the action of

   (a) ATP

   (b) Phosphorylase

   (c) Myosinage

   (d) Electrophoresis.

45. If a muscles is fatigued, the substance that accumulates in it is

   (a) Pyruvic acid

   (b) ADP

   (c) Lactic acid

   (d) CO_2.

Answer sheet is at the end of the book.

Chapter 4

GENERAL PHYSIOLOGY

1. **The following glands secrete saliva except**

   (a) Lachrymal glands
   (b) Parotid glands
   (c) Submaxillary glands
   (d) Sublingual glands

2. **At the nerve endings, the hormone released is known as**

   (a) Gastrin
   (b) Enterogastrone
   (c) Acetylcholine
   (d) Sympathin.

3. **The disease pellagra is characterized by**

   (a) Gastro intestinal disorders
   (b) Disorders of endocrine glands
   (c) Disorders of the kidney
   (e) Malfunction of the liver.

4. **The production of blood cospuscles is called**

   (a) Erythropoiesis
   (b) Haemolysis
   (c) Ganulopoiesis
   (d) Haemopoiesis.

5. Biliverdin and bilirubin are excereted mainly along with

(a) Urine

(b) Faeces

(c) Sweat

(d) Vitamins

6. Pinocytosis implies

(a) Endocytosis of large particulate matter

(b) Extrusion of particles by the cell

(c) Endocytosis of protein macromolecules

(d) Digestion by the cell.

7. The enzymes are composed of

(a) Fibrillar proteins

(b) Neutral fats

(c) Globular proteins

(d) Carbohydrate moieties

8. The lipid layer of cell membrane is composed of

(a) Triglycerides

(b) Cholesterol and phospholipids

(c) Lipoproteins

(d) Free fatty acids.

9. The peroxisomes are important in

(a) Alcohol detoxification

(b) Synthesis of fatty acids

(c) Intracellular digestion

(d) Breakdown of glucose.

10. Amoeboid movement is present in

(a) All the cells

(b) RBCs

(c) Spherocytes

(d) Reticulocytes.

11. **Protein channels are associated with**

(a) Nuclear membrane

(b) Gating

(c) Non-selective nature of ion transport

(d) Passage of proteins into the ECF.

12. **Faciliated transport involves**

(a) Energy input

(b) Amino acids

(c) Tranfer against a concertratun gradient

(d) Pinocytosis.

13. **Simple diffusion is associated with**

(a) Unidirectional transport across the cell membrane

(b) Binding of carrier protein in the membrane

(c) Na^+ transport

(d) Absence of energy expenditure.

14. **Glucose is transported across the cell membrane by**

(a) Active transport

(b) Passive transport

(c) Facilitated transport

(d) Water channels.

15. **Renal excretion of potassium is markedly decreased during**

(a) Aldosterone administration

(b) Addison's disease

(c) Increased dietary potassium

(d) Thiazide administration.

16. Potassium depletion causes

(a) Altered cardiac rhythm

(b) Extra cellular metabolic acidosis.

(c) Intracellular alkalosis

(d) Enhanced contractility of smooth muscle.

17. Haemorrhage causes

(a) Enhanced renal perfusion

(b) Oliguria

(c) Reflex bradycardia

(d) Cutaneous vasodilation.

18. The anion gap increases during

(a) Diabetic ketoacidosis

(b) Metabolic alkalosis

(c) Hypoproteinaemia

(d) Renal tubular bicarbonate leak.

19. Plasma urea is increased by

(a) Increased GFR

(b) Sodium and water depletion

(c) Lowered protein intake

(d) Reduced protein catabolism.

20. Plasma albumin concentration decreases during

(a) Dehydration

(b) Anaemia

(c) Burns

(d) Nephrotic syndrome.

21. Abnormal response to valsalva's manoeuvre occurs in

(a) Underventilation

(b) Hyperventilation

(c) Histamine

(d) All of the above.

41. **The minor blood groups are**

(a) M

(b) N

(c) Rh

(d) All of the above.

42. **The commonest Rh antigen is**

(a) A

(b) B

(c) D

(d) AB.

43. **Haemolysis of blood is caused by**

(a) Quinine

(b) Ether

(c) Both of the above

(d) None of the above.

44. **The number of polypeptide chain in thrombin are**

(a) 1

(b) 2

(c) 3

(d) 4.

45. **Which of the following plays an important role in the transport of CO_2 in the blood ?**

(a) O_2

(b) CO_2

(c) Hh

(d) CO.

46. The scientist who discovered the blood groups based on group specific substances called A and B agglutinogen is

(a) Mendel

(b) Landsteiner

(c) Ross

(d) Wiener.

47. The group specific substance agglutinogen A is chemically

(a) Lipid-protein complex

(b) Protein with iron

(c) Carbohydrate and protein

(d) Polysaccharide.

48. A blood that contains the agglutinin called the anti-a will belong to

(a) A

(b) B

(c) AB

(d) O.

49. While the agglutinin is present in the serum, agglutinogen is present in

(a) RBC

(b) Plasma

(c) Serum

(d) WBC.

50. The discovery of Rh factor was done by injecting RBC from

(a) Rhesus monkey to man

(b) Man into Rhesus monkey

(c) Rabbit into rhesus monkey

(d) Rhesus monkey into rabbit.

51. In the case of woman with Rh-ve blood, the antibody present in her blood, before immunisation occurs is

(a) Rh^+ antibody

(b) Rh − antibody

(c) Mo antibody

(d) Rh^+ antibody.

52. In erythroblastosis foetalis, the antibodies **produced in the mother result in haemolysis of RBC which causes**

(a) Anaemia

(b) Jaundice

(c) Haemorrhage

(d) Histolyis.

53. The 'Universal Donor' belongs to blood group

(a) A

(b) B

(c) AB

(d) O.

54. Universal recipient belongs to group

(a) A

(b) B

(c) AB

(d) O.

55. In a normal man to help transport of O_2 and CO_2 properly the blood is

(a) Slightly alkaline

(b) Slightly acidic

(c) Strongly alkaline

(d) Strongly acidic.

56. **The production of antibodies on the injection of typhoid bacteria, which is called immunity is by**

  (a) The plasma

  (b) RBC

  (c) Spleen

  (d) Platelets.

57. **Antibodies are proteins of the type**

  (a) Albumins

  (b) γ -globulins

  (c) α - albumin

  (d) α - globulin.

Answer sheet is at the end of the book.

Chapter 6

CIRCULATORY SYSTEM

1. Though the heart is an involuntary organ the fibres are different from the smooth muscle fibres in possessing
   (a) Tendons
   (b) Sarcostyles
   (c) Sarcoplasm
   (d) Striations.

2. The similarity between voluntary muscle fibre and cardiac muscle fibre is that they are both
   (a) Syncytic
   (b) Branched
   (c) Unbranched
   (d) Nucleated.

3. The pacemaker is known as
   (a) Semi auricular node
   (b) Auriculo ventricular node
   (c) Bundle of His
   (d) Purkinje system.

4. The atrioventricular node is situated
   (a) Near the bicuspid valve
   (b) In between the atrium and ventricle
   (c) At the base of inter auricular septum
   (d) In the ventricular septum.

5. **In a normal resting man the rate of heart beat per minute is**

   (a) 60

   (b) 80

   (c) 70

   (d) 100

6. **In a normal man the amount of blood put out by the heart per minute is**

   (a) 4 litres

   (b) 5 litres

   (c) 1 litres

   (d) 3 litres.

7. **The rate of heart beat per minute is highest in the case of**

   (a) Man

   (b) Whale

   (c) Elephant

   (d) Mouse.

8. **The value between the left auricle and left ventricle is called the**

   (a) Tricuspid valve

   (b) Eustachian valve

   (c) Mitral valve

   (d) Semilunar valve.

9. **Foramen ovalis present only in the heart of embryos leads from the right auricle to**

   (a) Right ventricle

   (b) Post caval vein

   (c) Pulmonary artery

   (d) Left auricle.

10. **Eustachian valve which is of no significance in the adult mammal, is a vestigeal organ a vestige of**

   (a) Spiral valve

   (b) Sinus venosus

   (c) Sinauriciular valve

   (d) Semilunar valve.

11. **The nature of valve in the heart is**

   (a) Membranous

   (b) Muscular

   (c) Tendinous

   (d) Ligamentous.

12. **Since it is the sinuauricular node which initates the impulses, the heart of mammals is called**

   (a) Cholinergic

   (b) Adrenergic

   (c) Neurogenic

   (d) Myogenic.

13. **The main constituents of plasma proteins are**

   (a) Heparin

   (b) Fibrinogen

   (c) Globulin

   (d) Albumins.

14. **The number of RBC per cc of blood is about (in millions)**

   (a) 5.5

   (b) 7

   (c) 8

   (d) 3

15. The life span of RBC is
   (a) 40 days
   (b) 120 days
   (c) 80 days
   (d) 100 days.

16. The majority of the leucocyte in the blood are
   (a) Monocytes
   (b) Lymphocytes
   (c) Eosinophils
   (d) Phagocytes.

17. Thrombocytes last in the blood for about
   (a) 3 to 5 days
   (b) 1 week
   (c) 20 days
   (d) 3 to 6 days.

18. Monocytes are leucocytes which
   (a) Produce antitoxins
   (b) Produce toxin
   (c) Are phagocytes
   (d) Are non - phagocytes.

19. The lymph is mainly formed by
   (a) Lymph nodes
   (b) Lymph glands
   (c) Villi of intestine
   (d) Interstitial liquid.

20. The lympathic system joins the blood vascular system in the region of
   (a) Pulmonary artery
   (b) Systemic arch

(c) Precaval vein

(d) Sinuses of liver.

21. **The function of lymph glands is to**

   (a) Eliminate fat

   (b) Synthesize lymph

   (c) Intercept bacteria

   (d) Circulate lymph.

22. **The function of the lymphocytes is to**

   (a) Engulf bacteria

   (b) Help in clotting

   (c) Produce antitoxins

   (d) Transport lymph.

23. **Thrombocytes last in the blood of man for about**

   (a) 3-5 days

   (b) 3-7 days

   (c) 1 week

   (d) 8 days.

24. **The thromboplastin is present not only in the blood platelets but is also produced by**

   (a) Damaged tissues

   (b) Hepatic lobule

   (c) Bone marrow

   (d) Lymph nodes.

25. **The amount of thrombocytes in 1 cc of blood is about**

   (a) 200,00-400,000

   (b) 3,000,000

   (c) 10,000-20,000

   (d) 2,50,000

26. One of the factors responsible for clotting of the blood, the absence of which causes a disease called haemophilia is known as

    (a) Factor I
    (b) Factor VII
    (c) Factor VIII
    (d) Factor IX.

27. The precursor of prothrombin is a vitamin which may be synthesized by bacteria in the intestine. This vitamin is

    (a) Cynacobalmin
    (b) Naphthoquinone
    (c) Histamine
    (d) Heparin.

28. The site of production of blood platelets is

    (a) Liver lobules
    (b) Red bone marrow
    (c) White bone marrow
    (d) Malpighi of spleen.

29. The production of blood corpuscles is called

    (a) Erythropoiesis
    (b) Haemolysis
    (c) Granulopoiesis
    (d) Haemopoiesis.

30. The venom of Russels Viper may be scientifically used for haemophilia because it contains

    (a) Fibrinogen
    (b) Cations
    (c) Poisons
    (d) Thromboplastins.

31. **Rapidity of conduction is greatest in the**
    (a) Atrial muscle
    (b) Purkinge fibres
    (c) AV nodal region
    (d) Ventricular muscle.

32. **The cardiac sympathetic innervation is distributed to**
    (a) The SA and AV nodes
    (b) All parts of the heart
    (c) Ventricular muscle alone
    (d) Atrial musculature.

33. **The action potential is longer in the cardiac muscle because**
    (a) Fast sodium channels are present in the cardiac muscle
    (b) Potassium leak channels are present in the cardiac muscle
    (c) Potassium permeability is increased during the action potential
    (d) Slow clacium-sodium channels operates in the cardiac muscle.

34. **The myocardial depressant is**
    (a) Ca^{++}
    (b) Mg^{++}
    (c) Digitalis
    (d) Na^+.

35. **The cardiac muscle has the following properties except**
    (a) A prolonged action potential
    (b) Tetanus
    (c) Treppe
    (d) All of the above.

36. The fourth heart sound is associated with

(a) Physiologic ventricular filling

(b) Ventricular hypertrophy

(c) Normal young individuals

(d) A-V fistula.

37. Stimulation of the vagi supplying the heart causes

(a) Increased permeability of the fibre membrane to Na^+ and Ca^{++}

(b) Decreased atrio-ventricular conduction time

(c) Increased permeability of the fibre mebrane to K^+

(d) Increased positivity of the SA nodal resting membrane potential.

38. Re-entrant impulses occur in one of the following situations

(a) Administration of acetylcholine

(b) High blood potassium

(c) Constrictive pericarditis

(d) High blood sodium

39. Premature cardiac contraction is associated with

(a) Accetys cholind administration

(b) Overuse of nicotine

(c) Sleep

(d) Ca^{++} channel blockers

40. Tachycardia can be converted to normal sinus rhythm by

(a) Neuro muscular blockade

(b) Pressing on the eyeball

(c) Increasing the ECF Na^+ concentration

(d) Getting up from the recumbent position.

41. The P-R segment is lengthened in
(a) Sinus tachycardia
(b) A-V nodal disease
(c) Thyrotoxicosis
(d) Diminished serum K⁺

42. A tall P wave occurs in
(a) Atrial fibrillation
(b) Atrial flutter
(c) Excercise
(d) Hypothyrodism.

43. The rise of T wave is due to
(a) Ventricular depolarization
(b) Repolarization in the ventricular septum
(c) Atrial repolarization
(d) Depolarization of the right atrium.

44. A short P-R interval may be due to
(a) A-V nodal rhythm
(b) First degree AV block
(c) Digitalis administration
(d) Elevation of serum K⁺.

45. Cardiac output is decreased during
(a) Sleep
(b) Pregnancy
(c) Histamine release
(d) Sitting up from lying position.

46. The mean systemic pressure increases during
(a) Loss of sympathetic tone
(b) Muscular excercise
(c) Valsalva manoeuvre
(d) Loss of blood volume.

47. **Reduced peripheral resistance is seen in the following conditions except**

   (a) Beriberi

   (b) Arterio-venous fistula

   (c) Polycythemia

   (d) Hyperthyroidism.

48. **Venous return decreases during**

   (a) Acute venous dilation

   (b) Increased blood volume

   (c) Anaemia

   (d) Hyperthyroidism.

49. **Cardiac output is altered by the following factors except**

   (a) Preload

   (b) After load

   (c) Changes in the arterial pressure between 90-150 mm kg

   (d) Xanthine administration.

50. **Section of both the carotid sinus nerve causes**

   (a) Fall in diastolic blood pressure

   (b) Decrease in heart rate

   (c) Vasovagal syncope

   (d) Rise of systemic blood pressure.

51. **Clamping of the carotid astery above the carotid sinus causes**

   (a) Reflex fall in systemic BP

   (b) Reflex rise in BP

   (c) Increased peripheral resistance

   (d) Reflex tachycardia.

52. Increased left atrial pressure causes

(a) Vasoconstriction

(b) Diuresis

(c) Reflex bradycardia

(d) All of the above.

53. In humans in whom both noradrenergic and cholinergic systems are blocked, the heart rate is approximately

(a) 72/min.

(b) 50/min.

(c) 100/min.

(d) 180/min.

54. The cholinergic sympathetic vasodilator fibres are associated with

(a) Tonic activity

(b) Alarm action

(c) Craniosacral outflow

(d) Salivary glands.

55. Long term control of arterial pressure is through

(a) Carotid and aortic baroreceptors

(b) Pressure natriuresis

(c) Vasopressin

(d) Bainbridge reflex.

56. Mayer waves are caused by

(a) Respiration

(b) Tachycardia

(c) Increased PO_2

(d) Chemoreceptor discharge.

57. **Tolerance for 'g' forces is greatest in the case of**

(a) Chest-to-back direction

(b) Back-to-chest direction

(c) Positive g

(d) Negative g.

58. **On assuming the upright position there is**

(a) Bradycardia

(b) Arteriolar vasodilation

(c) Increase in renin and aldosterone

(d) All of the above.

59. **The effects of zero gravity is**

(a) Cardiac disuse atrophy

(b) Skeletal muscle hypertrophy

(c) Increase in EC+ volume

(d) Venous pooling in the extremities.

60. **A high blood flow in exercising muscle is caused by**

(a) Rise in tissue PO_2

(b) Increased sympathetic discharge

(c) Rise in PCO_2

(d) Rise in pH.

61. **During isometric exercise**

(a) Stroke volume increases

(b) Systolic and diastolic blood pressure increases

(c) Skeletal muscle blood flow increases

(d) Cardiac output may exceed 35 l/min.

62. **Moderate haemorrhage causes**

(a) Increase in pulse pressure

(b) Tachycardia

(c) Vasodilation

(d) ADH suppsession.

63. **The following brain area is outside the blood brain barrier**

(a) Pineal gland

(b) Cerebral cortex

(c) Anterior pitutary

(d) Basal ganglia.

64. **The most common site of myocardial infarction is**

(a) Left atrial muscle

(b) Epicardium

(c) Left ventricular subendocardium

(d) Right ventricular muscle.

65. **Coronary vasodilation is caused by**

(a) Hyperventilation

(b) Adenosine

(c) Ca^{++}

(d) Na^{++}.

66. **At birth the foe`tal circulation undergoes one amongst the following changes**

(a) Decrease in peripheral resistance

(b) Fall in pulmonary vascular resistance

(c) Increase in O_2 affinity of RBCs

(d) Decrease in left atrial pressure.

67. **Erythropoietin is stimulated by all except**

(a) Low blood volume

(b) Polycythaemia

(c) Poor blood flow

(d) Pulmonary disease.

68. The alternate pathway of complement system is associated with all except

(a) Antigen-antibody reactions

(b) Opsonization

(c) Chemotaxis

(d) Inflammatory effects

69. Turbulent flow of blood occurs in one of the following situations

(a) Reynolds number more than 3000

(b) Dilatation of an artery

(c) Polycythemia

(d) Velocities below the critical velocity.

70. Venous valves are present in

(a) Veins from the brain

(b) Limb veins

(c) Veins from the viscera

(d) Superior vena cava.

71. Angiogenesis is inhibited by

(a) Platelet derived growth factor

(b) Heparin

(c) Prostaglandins

(d) Bradykinin.

72. Peripheral resistance increases in

(a) Severe polycythemia

(b) Anaemia

(c) Acclimatization to high altitude

(d) Hypogammaglobulinaemia.

73. Atrial natriuretic peptide has the following actions except

(a) Activation of renin secretion

(b) Lowering of blood pressure

(c) Natriuresis

(d) Inhibition of ADH secretion.

74. Nitric acid is known to cause

(a) Arterial vasodilation

(b) Hypertension

(c) Atherosclerosis

(d) Contraction of GI tract smooth muscle.

75. Endothelins can cause

(a) Dilation of vascular smooth muscle

(b) Positive inotropic effect on myocardium

(c) Decrease in renal vascular resistance

(d) Bronchodilation.

76. Bradykinin has one of the following biological actions

(a) Contraction of visceral smooth muscle

(b) Contraction of vascular smooth muscle

(c) Relief of pain

(d) Decrease in capillary permeability

Answer sheet is at the end of the book.

Chapter 7

DIGESTIVE SYSTEM

1. **The enzyme found in the saliva is**
    (a) γ amylases
    (b) Ptyalin
    (c) Maltase
    (d) Pepsin

2. **The valve inbetween the oesophagus and the stomach is called**
    (a) Ileo-coelic valve
    (b) Gastric valve
    (c) Cardia
    (d) Sphincter

3. **The inner lining of the stomach is covered by an adherent mucoid alkaline substance which**
    (a) Serves for digestion of starch
    (a) Has bactericidal actions
    (c) Prevents the action of pesin on mucosa
    (d) Helps to continue the digestion of starch.

4. **Oxyntic cells secrete HCl while chief cells secrete**
    (a) Mucous
    (b) Pepsinogen
    (c) Pepsin
    (d) Mucous.

5.   **Optimum pH for the conversion of pepsinogen to pepsin is**

      (a) 2

      (b) 3

      (c) 1

      (d) 4.5

6.   **Peptic and oxyntic cells are found mostly in**

      (a) Fundus and Pylorus

      (b) Cardiac

      (c) Pylorus

      (d) Cardiac and pylorus.

7.   **The taste of food reflexly provokes gastric secretion by the stimulation of vagus nerve which ends in plexus called**

      (a) Meissner's

      (b) Coeliac

      (c) Infra coeliac

      (d) Sub-mucosal

8.   **At the nerve endings the hormone released is known as**

      (a) Gastrin

      (b) Enterogastrone

      (c) Acetylcholine

      (d) Sympathin.

9.   **The hormone gastrin is secreted by the**

      (a) Fundic region

      (b) Cardiac region

      (c) Pyloric antrum

      (d) Cardio - fundus

10. The following statements are true in relation to saliva except

(a) It contains an enzyme which is essential for complete digestion of starch

(b) Maintains mouth Ph around 7

(c) Helps in speech

(d) Has important lubricating action.

11. The carbohydrates in small gut are hydrolyzed by the following enzyme except

(a) Ptyalin

(b) Lactases

(c) Maltases

(d) Sucrases.

12. Which of the following statements is incorrect about saliva

(a) Prevent dental caries

(b) Helps in deglutition

(c) Is essential for the complete digestion of starch

(d) Prevents decalcification of the teeth.

13. Salivary secretion increases

(a) During motion sickness

(b) Just before vomiting

(c) More by bitter food than sweet one

(d) All of the above.

14. As the masticated food passes through the oesophagus

(a) Cardiac sphincter constricts

(b) Stomach shows receptive relaxation

(c) Pyloric sphincter relaxes

(d) All of the above.

15. **Gastric emptying is promoted by**

  (a) Decreased recreation of cholecystokinin

  (b) Presence of protein in the duodenum

  (c) Distension of duodenum

  (d) All of the above.

16. **Which of the following statements is incorrect for stomach. It**

  (a) Has less contractions half an hour after meal of solid food than when it is empty.

  (b) Absorbs over 30% of products of protein digestion

  (c) Produces gastric intrinsic factor

  (d) Depends on carbonic anhydrase for HCl production.

17. **Gastric secretions**

  (a) Are stimulated by histamine injection

  (b) Are enhanced by mere thought of food

  (c) Contain factor which helps in vit. B12 absorption.

  (d) All of the above.

18. **Apart from vagal stimulation the hormone gastrin is also secreted by the presence of**

  (a) HCl in the stomach

  (b) Unacted starch in the stomach

  (c) Meat in the stomach

  (d) Mucidous maltose in the stomach

19. **When fat is in the stomach the secretion of gastrin is inhibited. This inhibition is due to**

  (a) Presence of fat

  (b) Non stimulation of vagus

  (c) Slow digestion of fat

  (d) Release of enterogastrone.

20. **Effect of the reflex action due to the taste of food is the release of**

(a) Vagal impulses

(b) Appetite juice

(c) Alkaline mucous

(d) Spasms of stomach.

21. **In man, there are about 35,000,000 gastric pits at the rate of about**

(a) 200 per mm^2

(b) 300 per mm^2

(c) 1000 per mm^2

(d) 100 per mm^2.

22. **The pH of the panereatic juice is about**

(a) 6.4

(b) 8.4

(c) 12.0

(d) 7.0

23. **The pancreatic juice is secreted by the influence of a homone called secretin. But the juice is**

(a) Rich in HCO_3^- without enzyme

(b) Rich in enzymes, without anions

(c) In equal amounts of both

(d) Rich in enzymes without water.

24. **The hormone secretin is secreted by**

(a) Pyloric antrum

(b) Duodenum and jejunum

(c) Jejunum and ileum

(d) Stomach and duodenum.

25. The result of vagal stimulation of pancreas and the action of hormone are same ie., it results in the release of enzyme rich but low volume pancreatic juice. This hormone is known as

    (a) Cholecystokinin

    (b) Secretin

    (c) Pancreozymin

    (d) Acetylcholine.

26. The Brunner's glands of the duodenum secrete

    (a) An acidic juice to neutralize bile

    (b) An alkaline juice of enzymes

    (c) A juice only of enzymes

    (d) An alkaline juice rich in mucous.

27. The stomach

    (a) Motility increases when fats enter duodenum

    (b) Motility is inhibited by enterogastrone

    (c) Absorbs Vit B_{12}

    (d) Acid inhibits iron absorption

28. Gastric juice secretion

    (a) Is increased when food stimulates cells in pyloric region

    (b) In response to food ingestion is reduced if both vagi are cut

    (c) Is enhanced on histamine injection

    (d) All of the above.

29. Gastrin is characterized as linear peptide that

    (a) Increases gastric secretion

    (b) Is released by the stomach when it is distended

    (c) Is released in response to parasympathetic stimulation of stomach

    (d) All of the above.

30.   An increase in body fat

   (a) Decreases survival time in cold water
   (b) Favours survival in cold water
   (c) Increases specific gravity
   (d) Results in reduction of the lean body mass.

31.   A person suffering from hyperacidity of peptide ulcer is relieved by

   (a) Atropine
   (b) Cimetidine
   (c) Both A and B
   (d) None of the above.

32.   Man is unable to digest

   (a) Cellulose
   (b) Dextrin
   (c) Glycogen
   (d) Lactose

33.   Renin is

   (a) Secreted by JGA of kidney
   (b) Important for digestion of milk fats
   (c) Not found in man
   (d) None of the above.

34.   Dumping syndrome is mostly due to

   (a) Considerable rise in plasma kinin levels
   (b) Exaggerated fluctuation of blood glucose
   (c) Marked increase in lipid content of faeces
   (d) All of the above.

35.   Secretin is released from duodenal mucosa and it

   (a) Reduces gastric and duodenal motility
   (b) Increases mucus output from Bruners gland
   (c) Increases volume and electrolyte output of both
   (d) All of the above.

36. **The action of cholecystokinin is to**

    (a) Release bile from the liver

    (b) Make the enzyme alkaline

    (c) Contract the gall bladder

    (d) Activate Brunner's glands

37. **The oval Peyer's Patches found in the intestine produce WBCs, the function of which is**

    (a) Digestion of fat

    (b) Production of antitoxin

    (c) Production of lipase

    (d) Absorption of fat.

38. **Enterokinase secreted by the ileum acts on**

    (a) Trypsinogen

    (b) Succus entericus

    (c) Amylopsin

    (d) Lipase.

39. **One of the hormones that directly influences the role of absorption of glucose is**

    (a) Secretin

    (b) Cholecystokinin

    (c) Thyroxine

    (d) Pancreozymin.

40. **The fat present in the milk is readily digested by**

    (a) Intestinal lipase

    (b) Gastric lipase

    (c) Pancreatic lipase

    (d) None of the above.

41. **Lipase is activated by**

    (a) Secretin

    (b) Succus entericus

(c) Bile salts

(d) Enterokinase

42. **In an emulsion of fat the size of the fat droplets is**

(a) 0.05 mm

(b) 0.5 u

(c) 1.00 u

(d) 2.00 u

43. **The enzyme cellulase for the digestion of cellulose is secreted by**

(a) Large intestine

(b) Small intestine

(c) Vermiform appendix

(d) Intestinal bacteria.

44. **Bile contains fats such as**

(a) Falty acids and glycerol

(b) Glycocholate and taurocholate

(c) Lecithin and cholesterol

(d) Tocoferol and calciferol.

45. **The amino acid essential for growth which is not present in wheat is**

(a) Valine

(b) Arginine

(c) Glycine

(d) Lysine.

46. **The following are some of the gastro-intestinal hormones except**

(a) CCK-PZ

(b) GIP

(c) Motilin

(d) Chymotrypsin.

47. **Cholecystokinin-pancreozymin**

   (a) Increases small bowel motility

   (b) Causes contraction of gall bladder

   (c) Slows gastric emptying

   (d) All of the above.

48. **The following enzymes are present in the pancreatic juice except**

   (a) Trypsin

   (b) Chymotrypsin

   (c) Carboxypeptidase

   (d) Pepsin.

49. **Vitamin B$_{12}$ deficiency may result from**

   (a) Total gastrectomy or ileal resection

   (b) Following ileal resection

   (c) High dietary intake of phosphates

   (d) None of the above.

50. **Iron absorption in intestine is**

   (a) Dependent upon iron excretion

   (b) Enhanced by conversion of ferrous to ferric form

   (c) Improved by phytates

   (d) Regulated in accordance with the body need for iron.

51. **Succus entericus contains**

   (a) A substance which activates trypsinogen

   (b) Enzymes which break down strach

   (c) Enzymes which convert monosaccharides into simpler molecules

   (d) None of the above.

52. **The liver can synthesise following proteins except**

(a) Albumin

(b) Fibrinogen

(c) Prothrombin

(d) Gamma-globulin.

53. **Intrinsic factor which helps in absorption of Vit B$_{12}$ is produced by**

(a) Parietal cells of stomach

(b) Chief cells of stomach

(c) Beta cells of pancreas

(d) Liver cells.

54. **Liver is the only organ normally involved in**

(a) Synthesis of urea

(b) Synthesis of heparin

(c) Conversion of glycogen to glucose

(d) All of the above.

55. **In the intestinal chyme, final sugars normally found are**

(a) Galaclose and xylose

(b) Glucose and fructose

(c) Ribose and mannose

(d) Xylose and ribose

56. **The specific dynamic action of food**

(a) Causes an increase in metabolic rate after eating.

(b) Is the effect of sympathetic stimulation on metabolic rate.

(c) Is entirely to the work done in digestion of food.

(d) Is the effect of exercise on metabolic rate.

57. The hepatic cell

    (a) Can store viatmins like B_{12}, A, D

    (b) Can detoxify certain drugs

    (c) Inactivates certain harmones

    (d) All the above.

58. Absorption of fat in the intestine

    (a) Is complete even if lipase is absent

    (b) Occurs mainly in terminal ileum

    (c) Must occur normally for adequate absorption of Vit A, D and K

    (d) All of the above.

59. The upper one third portion of small intestine can absorb most of the following except

    (a) Pyrimidines

    (b) Bile salts

    (c) Electroytes

    (d) All of the above.

60. The absorption of

    (a) Most of the water we drink occurs in stomach

    (b) Vit B_{12} in our diet takes place in stomach and first part of small intestine

    (c) Most of the calcium occurs in the duodenum

    (d) Iron occurs in large gut

61. Chymotrypsinogen

    (a) Is secreted by stomach

    (b) Is converted to chymotrypsinogen by the action of trypsin

    (c) Uses starch as its primary substrate

    (d) Uses fats as its primary substrate.

62. **The defaecation reflex**

    (a) Is facilitated by food entering the stomach

    (b) Is eliminated by the paralysis of skeletal muscle.

    (c) Is eliminated by destruction of lumbar cord

    (d) All of the above.

63. **The protein present in wheat is**

    (a) Leucosin

    (b) Gelatin

    (c) Histamine

    (d) Taurine.

64. **The rate of absorption of amino acids is faster than the rate of diffusion. Therefore, they are absorbed by**

    (a) Osmotic gradient

    (b) Capillaries

    (c) Active transport

    (d) Ultra filtration.

65. **The long chain fatty acids are absorbed into the lacteals of the villus where they are converted at once into triglycerides by the additon of**

    (a) Glycerol

    (b) Cholesterol

    (c) Fatty acids

    (d) Phospholipid.

66. **The liver in mammals consists of five lobes of which the posterior most on the left side is known as**

    (a) Caudate lobe

    (b) Left lateral

    (c) Azygo lobe

    (d) Spigelion lobe.

67. The glissin's capsule contain

(a) Bile ducts

(b) Liver lobule

(c) Hepatic cords

(d) Sinusoids.

68. The macrophages present in the vascular capillaries of the liver are called

(a) Leukocytes

(b) Kupffer's cells

(c) Polymorphs

(d) Lymphocytes.

69. Toxic compounds absorbed through food are mainly

(a) Excreted by the kidney

(b) Sent to ileum along with bile

(c) Detoxified by liver

(d) Converted into useful substances.

70. Vitamin K is the precurser for the synthesis by the liver of

(a) Vitamin D

(b) Lymph

(c) Fibrinogen

(d) Prothrombin

71. The anti coagulant synthesized by the liver is

(a) Heparin

(b) Histamine

(c) Labile factor

(d) Stable factor.

72. Deamination of proteins ocurs in the

(a) Muscles

(b) Kidney

(c) Liver

(d) Spleen.

73. **In the embryo of mammals the RBCs are formed in the**

(a) Liver

(b) Bone marrow

(c) Spleen

(d) Cartilage.

74. **Bile to a certain extent influences the action of ileum because**

(a) It contains a hormone

(b) It stimulates peristalsis

(c) It neutralizes the enzymes

(d) It serves as an antiseptic.

75. **Bile is yellowish green because of**

(a) Glycocholate and taurocholate

(b) Biliverdin and bilirubin

(c) Remnants of WBCs

(d) Creatine and hippuric acid.

76. **The function of the colon is mainly to**

(a) Store bacteria

(b) Store faeces

(c) Absorb salts

(d) Absorb water.

77. **Ileocaecal sphincter contracts in response to**

(a) Stimulation of vagus

(b) Pentagastrin

(c) Secretin

(d) All of the above

78. **A most complete absorption of the following normally accurs in the small intestine**

    (a) Water

    (b) Vitamin B_{12}

    (c) Salts

    (d) All of the above.

79. **Breast feeding of an infant is advantageous because the milk**

    (a) Is nutritinally superior to any other alternative

    (b) Is the least allergeic of any infant food

    (c) Is bacteriologically safe and always fresh

    (d) All of the above.

80. **The breast feeding is contraindicated if**

    (a) Infant has galactosemia

    (b) Infant has phenylketouria

    (c) The mother is on drugs which pass into her milk

    (d) All of the above.

81. **Basal metabolic rate**

    (a) Is proportional to surface area

    (b) Increases in thyrotoxicosis

    (c) Can be estimated from carbon dioxide production if RQ is known

    (d) All of the above.

82. **Fat stores in the body**

    (a) Normally in the adult comprise 5% of body weight

    (b) Release fatty acid in response to insulin

    (c) Release fatty acids to adrenergic nerve

    (d) None of the above.

83. Serum cholesterol

   (a) Level rises in hypothyroidism

   (b) Level rises to increased amount of saturated fat intake

   (c) Is a precursor of adrenal cortical hormones

   (d) All of the above.

84. An increase in body fat

   (a) Favours survival in the cold water

   (b) Decreases survival in the cold water

   (c) Increases specific gravity of the body

   (d) None of the above.

85. The feeling of satiation results in response to following except

   (a) Distention of stomach

   (b) Rise in blood glucose level

   (c) Stimulation of lateral nucleus of hypothalamus

   (d) None of the above.

86. Contraction of intestinal smooth muscle may be influenced by the following except

   (a) Parasympathetic

   (b) Chemicals present in lumen

   (c) Somatic nerves

   (d) Enteric nerves.

87. Gastro intestinal peptides

   (a) Are often found in nerves of GI tract

   (b) Are all hormones

   (c) Are present in diverse endocrine organs

   (d) Have only one physiological action per peptide.

88. **GI smooth muscle cells**

    (a) Are each directly innervated

    (b) Are functionally coupled

    (c) Contain neuromuscular junctions

    (d) Are larger than skeletal muscle cells.

89. **Oesophageal peristalsis**

    (a) Is abolished by vagotomy

    (b) Is under hormonal control

    (c) Can occur in the absence of a swallow

    (d) Is not effective for liquids.

90. **The lower oesophageal sphincter**

    (a) Is a distinct ring of circular muscle.

    (b) Relaxes before a bolus arise

    (c) Consists of striated muscle

    (d) Is primarily under hormonal control.

91. **Receptive relaxatioin of stomach**

    (a) Is abolished by vagotomy

    (b) Occurs primarily in antrum

    (c) Results in large increase in 1/g pressure

    (d) None of the above.

92. **Gastric emptying**

    (a) Is more rapid for solids than liquids

    (b) Is stimulated by CCK

    (c) Is inhibited when acid enters duodenum

    (d) All of the above.

93. **Small gut contractions**

    (a) Are enhanced by parasympathetic activity

    (b) Are triggered by slow waves

   (c) Are absent in fasting man

   (d) Are primarily porpulsive in fed man.

94. The ileococal sphincter

   (a) Relaxes when ileum is distended

   (b) Relaxes when proximal colon is distended

   (c) Pressure is under hormonal control

   (d) Constricts when the pressure in ileum increases.

95. Which of the following would not be found in micelles

   (a) Chenodeoxycholate

   (b) Vitamin K

   (c) Bilirubin glucuronide

   (d) Lecithin.

96. Antral gastrin release is increased by

   (a) Somatostatin

   (b) Fat in the antrum of stomach

   (c) Protein digestion products in antrum

   (d) Secretin infusion.

97. Micelles are necessary for normal absorption of following except

   (a) Vitamin K

   (b) Medium chain fatty acid

   (c) Long chain monoglycerides

   (d) Dietary cholesterol.

98. Iodopsin which is also synthesized from vitamin A is found in

   (a) Cones

   (b) Rods

   (c) Thyroid

   (d) Blood

99. **Vitamin A is concerned with vision because it is converted into**

    (a) Xerophthol

    (b) β 'carotene

    (c) Retinol

    (d) Rhodopsin.

Answer sheet is at the end of the book.

Chapter 8

VITAMINS

1. **Which of the following Vitamins is associated with synthesis of coagulation factor pro-thrombin.**
    (a) Vitamin A
    (b) Vitamin C
    (c) Vitamin K
    (d) Vitamin E.

2. **Increased protein intake is accompanied by an increased dietary requirement for**
    (a) Ascorbic acid
    (b) Nicotinic acid
    (c) Pantothenic acid
    (d) Folic acid.

3. **The disease pellagra is due to a deficiency of**
    (a) Vitamin B6
    (b) Nicotinic acid
    (c) Pantothenic acid
    (d) Folic acid.

4. **Vitamin K2 was originallly isolated from**
    (a) Soyabeans
    (b) Putrid fish meal
    (c) Alfa - Alfa
    (d) Oysters.

5.   The following form of Vitamin A is use in the visusal cycle of wald
   (a) Retinol
   (b) Retinoic acid
   (c) Retinaldehyde
   (d) Retinyl acetate.

6.   Pantothenic acid exists in the tissues as
   (a) B – mercaptoethylamine
   (b) Coenzyme A
   (c) Pantonic acid
   (d) B – alanine.

7.   Patothenic acid deficiency cauases
   (a) Nausea
   (b) Irritability
   (c) Anaemia
   (d) All of the above.

8.   The normal concentration of riboflavin in plasma in μg/100 ml is
   (a) 1.5 to 3.5
   (b) 2.5 to 4.0
   (c) 3.5 to 5.5
   (d) 4.5 to 7.5

9.   Riboflavin is involved in the regulatory function of some hormones connected with the metabolism of
   (a) Carbohydrate
   (b) Fat
   (c) Protein
   (d) Minerals.

10.   FMN is a constituent of the
   (a) Warbrurg yellow enzyme
   (b) Cytochrome C reductase
   (c) L amino acid dehydrogenase
   (d) All of the above.

11. Niacin is present in maize in the form of

(a) Niatin

(b) Niacytin

(c) Nicyn

(d) Nicotin.

12. The normal concentration of niacin in the blood is

(a) 0.3 to 0.5 mg/100 ml

(b) 0.6 to 0.99 mg/10 ml

(c) 0.5 to 0.8 mg/100 ml

(d) All of the above.

13. Nicotinic acid is essential for the normal functioning of

(a) Skin

(b) Intestinal tract

(c) Nervous system

(d) All of the above.

14. Pyridoxine is a mixture of

(a) Pyridoxine

(b) Pyridoxal

(c) Pyridoxamine

(d) All of the above.

15. Pyridoxine produces a coloured compound with

(a) 2.6 dichloro quinone

(b) 2.4 nitroquinone

(c) 2.6 dichloroquinone

(d) All of the above.

16. **Pyriodoxal phosphate is involved in the desulphuration of**

    (a) Cysteine

    (b) Homocysteine

    (c) Both of the above

    (d) None of the above.

17. **Pyroxine deficiency causes**

    (a) Lymphopenia

    (b) Peripheral neuropathy

    (c) Both of the above

    (d) None of the above.

18. **Retinal is reduced to retinol by retinene reductase in presence of the coenzyme**

    (a) NAD^+

    (b) NAD^+ NADP

    (c) $NADH^+$ H^+

    (e) $NADPH^+$ H^+

19. **Retinol exists as an ester with higher fatty acids in the**

    (a) Kidney

    (b) Liver

    (c) Lung

    (d) All of the above.

20. **Carotenes are transported with the**

    (a) Proteins

    (b) Lipids

    (c) Lipoproteins

    (d) Minerals.

21. The dietary Vitamin A which is hydrolyzed in the lumen of the intestine by the enzyme

(a) Peptidase

(b) Lipids

(c) Nuclease

(d) Amylase.

22. In the blood vitamin esters are attached to

(a) Peptidase

(b) Lipase

(c) Nuclease

(d) Amylase.

23. The percentage of vitamin A in the form of esters stored in the liver is

(a) 70

(b) 80

(c) 90

(d) 95.

24. The preformed vitamin A is supplied by foods such as

(a) Butter

(b) Fish liver oil

(c) Eggs

(d) All of the above.

25. The poor source of vitamin D is

(a) Liver

(b) Eggs

(c) Milk

(d) Butter.

26. The normal concentration of vitamin D in blood in IU/L is

(a) 600 – 2500

(b) 700 - 3100

(c) 800 - 4100

(d) `850 – 4700

27. The activity of tocopherols is destroyed by

(a) Oxidation

(b) Reductioin

(c) Conjugation

(d) All of the above.

28. Some tocopherols are

(a) Terpenoid in structure

(b) Farnesyl in structure

(c) Dionol in structure

(d) Isoprenol in structure.

29. The methyl groups in the aromatic nucleus of tocopherol are

(a) 2

(b) 3

(c) 4

(d) 5

30. Vitamin E is stored in

(a) Mitochondria

(b) Microsomes

(c) Both of the above

(d) None of the above.

31. Vitamin K regulates the synthesis of blood clotting factors

(a) VII

(b) IX

(c) X

(d) All of the above

32. **The poor sources of Vitamin K 1 are**

(a) Fish

(b) Meat

(c) Milk

(d) All of the above.

33. **Vitamin E protects enzymes from destruction in**

(a) Nerves

(b) Muscles

(c) Gonads

(d) All of the above.

34. **The tocopherols prevent the oxidation of**

(a) Vitamin A

(b) Vitamin C

(c) Vitamin D

(d) Vitamin K.

35. **Vitamin E protects the polyunsaturated fatty acids from oxidation by molecular oxygen in the formation of**

(a) Trioxide

(b) Peroxide

(c) Superoxide

(d) All of the above.

36. **One IU is equal to the number of micrograms of B carotene**

(a) 0.3

(b) 0.4

(c) 0.6

(d) 0.8

37. **The nonprotein part of rhodopsin is**

(a) Retinal

(b) Carotene

(c) Retinol

(d) Repsin.

38. **The normal concentration of vitamin A in blood in IU/dl**

(a) 30-55

(b) 24-60

(c) 40-65

(d) 35-70

39. **Continued intake of excessive amounts of vitamin A especially in children produces**

(a) Irritability

(b) Headache

(c) Anorxeia

(d) All of the above.

40. **Vitamin D 2 is also called as**

(a) Activated ergosterol

(b) Ergocalciferol

(c) Viosaterol

(d) All of the above.

41. **Ascorbic acid can reduce**

(a) 2,6 dichlorophenolindophenol

(b) 2,6 dibromobenzene

(c) 2,4 dinitrobenzene

(d) 2 dioxypyridine.

42. **Sterilized milk is devoid of**
    (a) Vitamin D
    (b) Vitamin A
    (c) Vitamin C
    (d) Vitamin B.

43. **Vitamin C is required in the metabolism of**
    (a) Tryptophan
    (b) Phenylalanine
    (c) Both of the above
    (d) None of the above.

44. **The symptoms of scurvy are**
    (a) Poor healing of wounds
    (b) Loosening of teeth
    (c) Anaemia
    (d) All of the above.

45. **Thiamine is also said to be**
    (a) Antiberiberi substance
    (b) Aneurine
    (c) Antineuritic vitamin
    (d) All of the above.

46. **Lipoic acid is also termed as**
    (a) Thioctic acid
    (b) Acetate replacement factor
    (c) Protogen
    (d) All of the above.

47. **Folic acid is also termed as**
    (a) Pteroyl – glutamic acid
    (b) SLR factor
    (c) Liver lactobacillus casei factor
    (d) All of the above.

48. **Thiamine is oxidised to thiochrome in alkaline solution by**

(a) Potassium dichromate

(b) Potassium ferricyanide

(c) Potassium permanganate

(d) Potassium chlorate.

49. **The requirement of Vitamin B1 is increased when metabolism is elevated as in**

(a) Hyperthyroidism

(b) Fever

(c) Increased muscular activity

(d) All of the above.

50. **Riboflavin in alkaline solution when exposed to UV light is converted into lumiflavin which in UV light has**

(a) Greenish yellow fluorescence

(b) Light yellow fluorescence

(c) Bluish yellow fluorescence

(d) Reddish yellow fluorescence.

51. **The vitamins which are the component of electron transport chain are**

(a) Niacinamide

(b) Riboflavin

(c) Both of the above

(d) None of the above.

52. **Provitamin form of vitamin A is**

(a) Pyridoxine

(b) Niacin

(c) Carotenes

(d) None of the above.

53. Vitamin B2 is also called as

(a) Riboflavin

(b) Pyridoxine

(c) Carotene

(d) None of the above.

Answer sheet is at the end of the book.

Chapter 9

EXCRETORY SYSTEM

1. The functional unit of the kidney is called the nephron or uriniferous tubule and each kidney possesses
    (a) 1 million tubules
    (b) 5 million tubules
    (c) 10,000 tubules
    (d) 50,000 tubules.

2. Bowman's capsule and glomerulus together constitute the
    (a) Malpighian tubule
    (b) A nephron
    (c) Malpighian corpuscle
    (d) Nephric corpuscle.

3. The proximal convoluted tubule has a brush border which is due to
    (a) Microvilli
    (b) Minute hairs
    (c) Endothelium
    (d) Folded tube.

4. The malplighian corpuscles lies in
    (a) Medulla
    (b) Liver
    (c) Cortex
    (d) Pelvis

5. **The collecting tubules lead into ducts called**

   (a) Tertiary duct

   (b) Ducts of Bellini

   (c) Henle's loop

   (d) Bowman's duct.

6. **Apart from urea, the other ammonia compound excreted is**

   (a) NH_4^+

   (b) NH_4OH

   (c) NH_4Cl

   (d) NH_3.

7. **An example of uricoletic animal which pridominantly excretes uric acid is**

   (a) Fish

   (b) Moth

   (c) Crab

   (d) Newt.

8. **Uricotelism is a method of conserving**

   (a) Na^+ and K^+

   (b) Space

   (c) Water

   (d) Energy.

9. **Those animals which excrete a large amount of NH_3 are**

   (a) Terrestrial

   (b) Egg- laying

   (c) Amphibians

   (d) Aquatic.

10. A substance which is actively secreted by renal tubules cannot be helpful in determining

   (a) Renal blood flow

   (b) Glomerular filtration rate

   (c) Filtration fraction

   (d) Renal plasma flow.

11. The term threshold substance implies that

   (a) There is no active secretion of that substance

   (b) There is no acitve reabsorption of that substance

   (c) There is no tubular maximum for secretion

   (d) None of the above.

12. Plasma clearance will be maximum for

   (a) Sodium

   (b) Bicarbonate

   (c) Phosphate

   (d) Calcium.

13. Plasma clearance will be the lowest for

   (a) Glucose

   (b) Urea

   (c) Uric acid

   (d) Insulin.

14. PAH clearance would indicate

   (a) GFR and renal blood flow

   (b) GFR and filtration fraction

   (c) GFR and tabular maximum

   (d) Renal blood flow.

15. **A substance that has a renal clearance 25 times that of insulin is probably**

   (a) Synthesized in tubules and secreted actively

   (b) Only filtered at glomerular level

   (c) Only secreted by renal tubules

   (d) Filtred and reabsorbed.

16. **GFR is increased in response to**

   (a) Rise in arterial blood pressure

   (b) Decrease in colloid osmotic pressure

   (c) Decrease in hydrostatic pressure in Bowman's capsule

   (d) All of the above.

17. **In a healthy individual usually GFR is**

   (a) 5% of the effective renal blood flow

   (b) Between 15-20% of the effective blood flow

   (c) Between 40-50% of the effective blood flow

   (d) Between 70-80% of the effective blood flow.

18. **The juxtamedullary nephrons**

   (a) Form more than 40% of the total nephrons

   (b) Have shorter loop of Henle

   (c) Lie solely in the renal medulla

   (d) None of the above.

19. **As the filtrate enter the collecting duct it may be having**

   (a) Same osmolarity as plasma

   (b) Less osmolarity as plasma

   (c) Both A and B

   (d) None of the above.

20. **Active reabsorption of glucose from the filtrate occurs in**

   (a) Proximal tubules

   (b) Collecting ducts

(c) Loop of Henle

(d) Juxtaglomerular apparatus.

21. **The percentage of concentratioin in mg in urine is maximum for**

(a) Glucose

(b) Urea

(c) Uric acid

(d) Insulin.

22. **Aldosterone causes an increase in**

(a) Sodium reabsorption from renal tubules

(b) Extracellular fluid volume

(c) Sodium / Potassium ratio of extracellular fluid

(d) All of the above.

23. **In the absence of ADH**

(a) There would be no water absorption in renal tubule

(b) Facultative water absorption is increased

(c) Facultative water absorption is decreased

(d) Obligatory water absorption is decreased.

24. **ADH**

(a) Inhibits the countercurrent mechanism

(b) Facilitates the countercurent exchange mechanism

(c) Increases tubular permeability of water

(d) Increases secretion of electrolytes in tubules.

25. **The proximal convoluted tubules**

(a) Are involued in obligatory water absorption

(b) Reabsorb all the glucose in the glomerular filtrate

(c) Reabsorb most of the electrolytes

(d) All of the above.

26. **The collecting ducts**

(a) Determine to a large extent the final osmolarity of urine

(b) Are rendered inpermeable to water by ADH

(c) Can secrete water molecules actively into the urine

(d) None of the above.

27. **Aldosterone**

(a) Is adrenal medullary hormone concerned with sodium retention

(b) Is produced mainly in the juxtaglomerular apparatus

(c) Increases sodium reabsorption in the tubules

(d) Increases potassium reabsorption in the tubules.

28. **The urea**

(a) Level in blood is normally maintained to the level from 20- 40 mg% with the help of kidneys

(b) Load when increases and presented to the nephron causes osmotic diuresis

(c) Rises in concentration as the filtrate passes down the tubule

(d) All of the above.

29. **The renal clearance**

(a) Of insulin provides an estimate of GFR

(b) Of phosphate is decreased by parathormone

(c) Of phosphate is increased by calcitonin

(d) None of the above.

30. **As fluid passes down the proximal convoluted tubules**

(a) Urea concentration falls

(b) Concentration of amino acid rises

(c) Concentration of sodium rises

(d) Flow velocity falls.

31. **All of the following statements in relation to aldosterone are correct except**

(a) It is secreted in large amounts when blood volume falls

(b) Its secretion tends to increase renal arterial pressure

(c) It is polypeptide in nature

(d) Its secretion results in a reduction in urinary volume.

32. **Potassium**

(a) Ions are reabsorbed in the proximal convoluted tubules

(b) Transport is blocked by aldosterone

(c) Reabsorption in tubules is insulin dependent

(d) Transport from the lumen of the nephron depends on Na^+ transport.

33. **Glucose**

(a) Reabsorptioin is most marked in distal convoluted tubules

(b) Transport is primarily by active secretion into tubular fluid

(c) Transport from the lumen of the nephrons depends on the Na^+ transport

(d) Transport is blocked by aldosterone.

34. **The major source of urea is**

(a) Dietary proteins

(b) Dietary purines

(c) Dietary pyrimidines

(d) Beta hydroxy butyric acid.

35. **Sodium content of the urine decreases**

(a) During osmotic diuresis

(b) Following administration of the hydrocortisone

(c) During chlorothiazide induced diuresis

(d) None of the above.

36. **In a patient of diabetes insipidus urine formed is**

 (a) Plenty with zero osmolarity

 (b) Hypertonic to plasma

 (c) Hypotonic to plasma

 (d) Isotonic to plasma.

37. **A patient of diabetes insipidus**

 (a) Produces urine which is hypotonic

 (b) Excretes urine with a specific gravity below 1.005

 (c) Have intracellular fluid with low osmolarity

 (d) None of the above.

38. **In chronic renal failure**

 (a) Anaemia occurs which seems to be of iron deficiency type

 (b) Plasma PCO_2 tends to be low

 (c) Specific gravity of urine is high

 (d) All of the above

39. **A patient getting carbonic anhydrase inhibitor drug is likely to show**

 (a) An increase in urinary volume

 (b) Increased loss of potassium in urine

 (c) A fall in plasma bicarbonate

 (d) All of the above.

40. **Cutting of sympathetic nerves to bladder may cause**

 (a) Retention of urine

 (b) Loss of pain sensation from bladder

 (c) Retention with overflow

 (d) None of the above.

41. Hypertensive patient receiving aldosterone antagonisty will show

(a) Decrease in urine output

(b) Decrease in blood volume

(c) Decrease in blood viscosity

(d) All of the above.

42. A patient with long standing prostatic enlargement is likely to show

(a) Hypertrophy of bladder

(b) Dilation of ureters

(c) Tendency towards urinary infection

(d) All of the above.

43. A long standing increase in the arterial PCO_2 is likely to cause

(a) A decrease in plasma concentration of potassium ions

(b) An increase in plasma bicarbonate

(c) A decrease in the amount of ammonium salts in urine

(d) None of the above.

44. Water diuresis is commonly seen in patients suffering from

(a) Diabetes mellitus

(b) Cushing syndrome

(c) Addisons disease

(d) Diabetes insipidus.

45. Which of the following leads to an increase in GFR

(a) An increase in plasma colloid osmotic pressure

(b) An increase in proximal tubular pressure

(c) An increase in ultrafiltration coefficient

(d) An increase in afferent arteriolar resistance.

46. **Which of the following is associated with decreased plasma angiotensin II levels**

   (a) A fall in Ca^+ activity in juxtaglomerular cells

   (b) Converting enzyme inhibition

   (c) High plasma angiotensin I level

   (d) Renin release.

47. **Which of the following would act to decrease GFR and renal blood flow**

   (a) Autoregulation

   (b) An increase in afferent arteriolar resistance

   (c) Prostaglandin E2

   (d) A decrease in afferent arteriolar resistance.

48. **Which of the following substances is not reabsorbed by a Tm- limited mechanism**

   (a) Glucose

   (b) Urea

   (c) Amino acids

   (d) Lactate.

49. **Which of the following segments show highest urea permeability**

   (a) Descending loop of Henle

   (b) DCT

   (c) Outer medullary collecting duct

   (d) Papillary collecting duct.

50. **In which region of the nephron is the tubular fluid always hypotonic to plasma by at least 10 mosmol / LH_2O**

   (a) Collecting duct

   (b) Cortical portion of thick ascending limb of loop of Henle

(c) Thin descending limb of loop of Henle

(d) DCT.

51. **In a reference man of 70 kg wt, Na⁺ ingestion per day varies in range**

(a) 100-250 mEq

(b) 0.02 –0.2 mEq

(c) 1.5 – 2.5 mEq

(d) 5-10 mEq.

52. **Which of the following factors favours increased aldosterone secretion**

(a) Hyokalaemia

(b) Low plasma renin level

(c) Dehydration

(d) Hypernatremia.

53. **As urine flows from the end of PCT to the tip of loop of Henle, the luminal Na⁺ concentration**

(a) Increases

(b) Decreases

(c) Remains unchanged

(d) None of the above.

54. **The thick ascending limb of loop of Henle absorbs approximately what percent of total filtered Na⁺ load**

(a) 10

(b) 1-10

(c) 25

(d) 67.

55. **Which of the following cations normally has the greatest fractional excretion rate**

(a) Na⁺

(b) K⁺

(c) Mg⁺

(d) Either K⁺ or Mg⁺ depending on dietary intake.

56. Glomeruli are located

(a) Only in the superficial renal cortex

(b) Only in the outer renal medulla

(c) Throughout the renal cortex

(d) Only in juxtamedullary cortex.

57. The following segment of the nephron are found only in the medulla

(a) Vasa recta

(b) Collecting duct

(c) Thin ascending limbs of loop of Henle

(d) Proximal straight tubule and thin.

58. Which of the following is not found in JGA

(a) Renin

(b) Specialised smooth muscle cells

(c) Macula densa cells

(d) Glomerular capillary loops.

Answer sheet is at the end of the book.

Chapter 10

RESPIRATORY SYSTEM

1. **The respiratory quotient is the ratio of**
   (a) Volume of oxygen absorbed to CO_2 evolved per unit time
   (b) Volume of CO_2 evolved to O_2 aborbed per unit time
   (c) Minute volume to tidal volume
   (d) O_2 consumption per minute to minute volume.

2. **During normal inspiration**
   (a) Intrathoracic pressure falls
   (b) Intrapulmonary pressure falls
   (c) Intraabdominal pressure rises
   (d) All of the above.

3. **An act of quiet inspiration**
   (a) Increases venous return to the heart
   (b) Involves less muscular effort than expiration
   (c) Begins when intrapleural pressure falls below atmospheric pressure
   (d) Is assisted by surface tension forces in the alveoli.

4. **In the pulmonary circulation**
   (a) Blood flow tends to be diverted from poorly ventilated to well ventilated alveoli
   (b) Local rise in PCO_2 causes vasodilation
   (c) Carbonic achydrase catalyzedbreakdown of carbonic acid to H_2O and CO_2
   (d) Haemoglobin gives off hydrogen ions.

5. **Coughing involves**

    (a) Integration in the cerebral cortex

    (b) Spasmodic contraction of the diaphragm

    (c) Closure of the epiglottis

    (d) Stimulation of hypoglossal nerve.

6. **Breathing under positive pressure causes**

    (a) Reduction in cardiac output

    (b) Tachycardia

    (c) Increased venous return to heart

    (d) Increased blood flow to lungs.

7. **The rhythm of respiration**

    (a) Requires activation from pontine centres

    (b) Originates primarily from expiratory centres

    (c) Persists after both the vagi are severed

    (d) All of the above.

8. **The followings can be measured with spirometer except**

    (a) Tidal volume

    (b) Inspiratory reserve volume

    (c) Vital capacity

    (d) Functional residual capacity.

9. **The maximum volume of air that can be expelled out forcefully after maximum inspiration is called as**

    (a) Tidal volume

    (b) Minute volume

    (c) Vital capacity

    (d) Functional residual capacity.

10. **The largest of the following lung volume/capacity is**

    (a) Tidal volume

    (b) Residual volume

    (c) Vital capacity

    (d) Functional residual capacity.

11. **Total lung capacity is**

   (a) Tidal volume plus residual volume

   (b) Residual volume plus vital cpacity

   (c) Expiratory reserve volume plus residual volume

   (d) Inspiratory capacity plus residual volume.

12. **The surfactant lining the lung alveoli**

   (a) Increases the compliance of the lungs

   (b) Reduces the surface tension of the alveolar fliud

   (c) Prevents the collapse of the alveoli

   (d) All of the above.

13. **In normal lungs**

   (a) Physiological dead space is always greater than anatomical dead space.

   (b) Dead space volume may increase by more than half during a maximal inspiration

   (c) Oxygen transfer can always be explained by passive diffusion

   (d) All of the above.

14. **Constriction of bronchial smooth muscle can result from the following except**

   (a) Cold stimulus to bronchial mucosa

   (b) A decrease in PCO_2 in bronchial air

   (c) Irritation of bronchial mucosa

   (d) Stimulation of local beta adrenoreceptors.

15. **The diffusion capacity of a gas across alveolocapilliary barrier**

   (a) Is greatest for oxygen than CO_2

   (b) Remains constant during exercise

   (c) Is unaffected if one lung is removed

   (d) Is usually expressed as vol per unit time per unit pressure gradient.

16. **The residual volume of the lung**
    (a) Is air remaining in the lungs after full expiration
    (b) Is to the tune of 4-5 litres
    (c) Decreases with age
    (d) Can be measured by spirometry.

17. **An increase in ventilation can be expected in the following except when**
    (a) Person goes to sleep
    (b) pH of CSF falls
    (c) Plasma bicarbonate level falls
    (d) Person is under physical stress.

18. **If peripheral chemoreceptor responses are lost**
    (a) A person is less able to adopt to life at high altitude
    (b) A 75% fall in PO_2 will not appreciably alter ventilation
    (c) A 10% rise in PCO_2 will not appreciably alter ventilatioin
    (d) Ventilation will not increase in exercise.

19. **The work of breathing**
    (a) Is inversely related to lung compliance
    (b) Is decreased when subject lies down
    (c) Remains constant during exercise
    (d) Is dependent of the rate of breathing for a given alveolar ventilation rate.

20. **Respiratory dead space**
    (a) Increases during coughing
    (b) Decreases when the blood adrenaline level rises
    (c) Removes all particulate matter from the inspired air before it reaches alveoli
    (d) Saturates the air with water vapour before it reaches the alveoli.

21. **Vital capacity**

    (a) Is greater in men than women of the same age and height

    (b) Can be measured by spirometry

    (c) Is equal to sum of inspiratory capacity and expiratory reserve volume

    (d) All of the above.

22. **The level of O_2 and CO_2 would rise and fall markedly with each respiration were it not for the**

    (a) Tracheal dead space

    (b) Residual volume

    (c) Expiratory reserve volume

    (d) Inspiratory reserve volume.

23. **The percentage of maximum breathing capacity which approximates the minute respiratory volume is about**

    (a) 90

    (b) 60

    (c) 25

    (d) 4

24. **From the pressure volume curve of the lungs during active respiration and static state one can measure**

    (a) Compliance only

    (b) Airway resistance only

    (c) Viscous resistance

    (d) All of the above.

25. **The lowest PO_2 is found in**

    (a) Expired air

    (b) Venous blood

    (c) Atmospheric air

    (d) Alveolar air.

26. **Oxygen extraction from the lungs may be facilitated by**

    (a) Low PO_2 of pulmonary artery blood

    (b) Increased pulmonary artery flow

    (c) Increased blood flow through alveolar capillaries

    (d) All of the above.

27. **Nitrogen washout or single breath oxygen method directly measures**

    (a) Residual volume

    (b) Functional residual capacity

    (c) Total lung capacity

    (d) Inspiratory capacity.

28. **The partial pressure of gases in the body of an individual descending below the sea will**

    (a) Increase linearly

    (b) Increase exponentially

    (c) Remain constant

    (d) Decrease linearly.

29. **Decompression syndrome is mainly characterized by symptoms which**

    (a) Are not associated with permanent damage

    (b) Include paralysis

    (c) Are painless

    (d) Will occur whenever nitrogen pressure inside the body is greater than outside the body.

30. **The direct effect of CO_2 on respiratory centre**

    (a) Can cause 8 fold increase in alveolar ventilation

    (b) Is ten times more than its effect via peripheral chemoreceptors.

(c) Constitutes the normal control of respiration

(d) All of the above.

31. **The effect of hypoxia on resperation**

   (a) Is mediated by its direct influence on respiratory centre

   (b) Can triple alveolar ventilation

   (c) Is seldom of physiological importance

   (d) Is prevented by lowering PCO_2

32. **When both the vagi are cut respiratory rate**

   (a) Increases

   (b) Decreases

   (c) Ceases

   (d) Remains constant.

33. **Chemical regulation of resperation is maximally affected by**

   (a) O_2

   (b) CO_2

   (c) H^+ ions

   (d) Lactic acid.

34. **The Herring Breurer reflex leads to**

   (a) Increased respiratory rate

   (b) Increased tidal volume

   (c) Prolonged inspiration

   (d) Poor alveolar respiration.

35. **Hyperpnoea during exercise is probably caused by**

   (a) Direct impulses from motor cortex

   (b) Decreased pH

   (c) Both of the above

   (d) None of the above.

36. **Stimulation of pontine apneustic centre causes**

   (a) Forceful expiration

   (b) Accelerated respiration

   (c) Forceful inspiration

   (d) Apnoea.

37. **Electrical stimulation of pneumotaxic centre leads to**

   (a) Forceful expiration

   (b) Acclerated respiration

   (c) Forceful inspiration

   (d) Apnoea.

38. **The percentage of total lung capacity which cannot be emptied out is about**

   (a) 50

   (b) 46

   (c) 24

   (d) 12

39. **As the blood passes through the systemic capillaries**

   (a) Its pH rises

   (b) Its oxygen dissociation curve shifts to the left

   (c) Carbonate ions pass from the RBC to the plasma

   (d) The concentration of chloride ions in RBC falls.

40. **CO_2 is transported in blood**

   (a) In dissolved form in plasma as bicarbonate

   (b) As bicarbonate

   (c) In combination with Hb

   (d) All of the above.

41. **A shift to the right in the oxygen dissociation curve occurs in the following except**

   (a) When temperature rises

   (b) When PCO_2 increases

(c) When foetal blood is replaced by adult blood

(d) In the pulmonary capillaries.

42. **Hyperbaric oxygen therapy may be toxic because it**

(a) Removes chemoreceptor drive of respiration

(b) Destroys certain enzymes

(c) Overstimulates oxidative chain of reactions

(d) Prevents Hb unloading of O_2 in tissues.

43. **Pure oxygen therapy can be of value in hypoxia due to**

(a) Carbon monoxide poisoning

(b) Diffusion defects

(c) Hypohaemoglobinaemia

(d) All of the above.

44. **Cyanosis is seen when concentration of**

(a) Deoxygenated Hb increases

(b) Deoxygenated Hb decreses

(c) Oxygenated Hb increases

(d) Oxygenated Hb decreases.

45. **The maximum amount of oxygen which can combine with a given amount of Hb varies with**

(a) PCO_2

(b) Temperature

(c) Concentration of Hb in blood

(d) None of the above.

46. **Bronchoconstriction due to bronchial asthma is likely to be relieved by**

(a) Acetylcholine

(b) Anticholinestrase drugs

(c) Beta adrenergic blockers

(d) Isoprenalin.

47. **Pneumothorax causes the following except**

  (a) A reduction in residual volume

  (b) A reduced vital capacity

  (c) Less obvious rib contours on the affected side

  (d) Abnormal dullness to percussion on affected side.

48. **A case of restrictive lung disease differs from obstructive disease in having a lower**

  (a) Residual volume

  (b) Vital capacity

  (c) Total lung capacity

  (d) All of the above.

49. **With optimal equipment the alveolar PCO_2 of a diver 33 feet below the surface is**

  (a) Normal

  (b) Half normal

  (c) Twice normal

  (d) Four times normal.

50. **A pilot involved in angular acceleration may**

  (a) Become hypotensive

  (b) Become unconscious

  (c) Fracture his vertebra

  (d) All of the above.

Answer sheet is at the end of the book.

Chapter 11

HORMONES

1. **Which of the following glands have definite endocrine functions**
    (a) Thymus
    (b) Pineal body
    (c) Thyroid
    (d) None of the above.

2. **Which of the following glands are with probable functions**
    (a) Pineal body
    (b) Thymus
    (c) Both of the above
    (d) None of the above.

3. **The hormones secreted by thyroid are**
    (a) Insulin
    (b) Thyroxin
    (c) Glycogen
    (d) ADH.

4. **Which of the following compounds interfere with organic incorporation of iodine.**
    (a) Thiourea
    (b) Thiouracil
    (c) Both of the above
    (d) None of the above.

5. The regulatioin of several enzymes as phospholipase A2, guanylate cyclase is dependent on

    (a) Ca^{2+}

    (b) Na^+

    (c) Mg^+

    (d) Fe^{2+}

6. Which of the following is not secreted by the anterior lobe of pituary gland

    (a) Growth

    (b) ACTH

    (c) ASH

    (d) None of the above.

7. Growth hormone is also a

    (a) Diabetogenic hormone

    (b) Neurohormone

    (c) Immunologic hormone

    (d) None of the above.

8. Which of the following is the tropic hormones secreted by pitutary gland

    (a) Corticotropin

    (b) Gonadotropin

    (c) Mammotropin

    (d) All of the above.

9. The conversion of primary spermatocytes into secondary spermatocytes in the seminiferous tubule is stimulated by

    (a) TSH

    (b) FSH

    (c) GH

    (d) LH.

10. **Posterior pituitary hormones are synthesized in**

(a) Neuro secretory neurons

(b) Neurons

(c) Neurophyseal cells

(d) None of the above.

11. **The rate limiting step in the biosynthetic pathway of catecholamines is**

(a) The hydroxylation of phenylalanine to tyrosine

(b) The decarboxylatioin of DOPA

(c) The reduction of biopterin

(d) The hydroxylation of tyrosine.

12. **Which of the following substances is present in high concentration in the urine of patients with phenochromocytomas**

(a) 3-methoxy-4-OH mandelic acid

(b) Epinephrine

(c) Metanephrine

(d) Nor epinephrine.

13. **Epinephrine is formed from nor-epinephrine by**

(a) N-methylation

(b) O-methylation

(c) Decarboxylation

(d) Hydroxylation.

14. **Which of the following abnormalities arise due to pituitary dysfunction**

(a) Acromegaly

(b) Gigantism

(c) Cushing disease

(d) All of the above.

15. **The principal hormones secreted by the follicular cells of thyroid are**

   (a) T4

   (b) T3

   (c) Reverse T3

   (d) All of the above.

16. **Thyroid hormones are synthesized from a protein called as**

   (a) Immunogen

   (b) Thyroglobulin

   (c) Thyroalbumin

   (d) None of the above.

16. **Thyroid hormones are synthesized from protein called as**

   (a) Immunogen

   (b) Thyroglobulin

   (c) Thyroalbumin

   (d) None of the above.

17. **Which of the following compete with iodide for uptake mechanism in thyroid gland.**

   (a) Thiocyanates

   (b) Perchlorates

   (c) Both of the above

   (d) None of the above.

18. **Which of the following is thyroxine binding protein and act as specific carrier agent for hormone**

   (a) Thyroxine binding globulin

   (b) Thyroxine binding prealbumin

   (c) Both of the above

   (d) None of the above.

Chapter 12

ENDOCRINE SYSTEM

1. **Negative feedback operates to control the secretion of**
   (a) Oxytocin
   (b) Cortisol
   (c) Parathormone
   (d) Both a and b.

2. **The hypothalamic releasing hormones have the following features**
   (a) Control of catecholamine secretion
   (b) Alteration of gene expression
   (c) Control of parathormone secretion
   (d) Regulation of gonadotraphin secretion.

3. **Steroid hormones are associated with**
   (a) Synthesizing ribosome
   (b) Are derived from cholesterol
   (c) Bind with cytoplasmic receptors
   (d) Both b and c.

4. **The following hormones exert their cellular effects through cycle AMP mechanism except**
   (a) ACTH
   (b) TSH
   (c) Catecholamines
   (d) Thyroid hormone.

5. **Second messenger mechanism is not employed in the case of**

    (a) Cholecalciferol

    (b) Catecholamines

    (c) TCH

    (d) Parathormone.

6. **The receptors are located in the cell membrane in the case of**

    (a) Testosterone

    (b) Tri-iodothyronine

    (c) Calcitonin

    (d) Thyroxine.

7. **The following are steroid hormone except**

    (a) Adrenal corticoids

    (b) Testosterone

    (c) Follice stimulating hormone

    (d) Oestrogens.

8. **One among the following hormones acts by decreasing cyclic AMP formation**

    (a) LH

    (b) LHRH

    (c) FSH

    (d) Somatostatin.

9. **In thyrotoxicosis the following effects are seen except**

    (a) Rise in blood glucose level

    (b) Lowering of cholesterol level

    (c) Decrease calorigenesis

    (d) Hyperphagia.

10. **Hypothyroidism has one of the following features**

    (a) Weight loss

    (b) Increased metabolic rate

    (c) Accumulation of proteins and polysaccharides

    (d) Protein catabolism

11. **Anti-thyroid agents include the following except**

    (a) Catecholamines

    (b) Perchlorate

    (c) Cabbages

    (d) Large doses of iodide.

12. **Thyroid hormones promote growth by**

    (a) Potentiating the effect of growth hormone

    (b) Accleration of chondrogenesis

    (c) Delaying epiphyseal closure

    (d) Increasing O_2 consumption.

13. **The thyroid gland is associated with the following features**

    (a) Immediate death on ablation

    (b) Stimulation of O_2 consumption of most body tissues

    (c) Heat intolerance on removal

    (d) Independent of hypothalmic control.

14. **The properties of thyroid hormone include**

    (a) Role in lipid metabolism

    (b) Growth and maturation in mammals

    (c) Both a and b

    (d) None of the above.

15. **Absence of thyroid hormones produce the following effects in the adult**
    (a) Cold intolerance
    (b) Accelerated calorigenesis
    (c) Negative nitrogen balance
    (d) None of the above.

16. **The action of 1,25-dihydroxy cholecalciferol includes**
    (a) Lowering of blood calcium
    (b) Deposition of calcium in the bone
    (c) Increased intestinal absorption of calcium
    (d) None of the above.

17. **Rickets can be caused by**
    (a) Inadequate intake of vitamin D
    (b) Inadequate exposure to sun
    (c) Kidney failure
    (d) All of the above.

18. **Calcitonin is associated with the following features**
    (a) Phosphate raising effect
    (b) Increased urinary calcium excretion
    (c) Causing bone resorption
    (d) Increased calcium reabsorption.

19. **Tetany is characterized by the following features**
    (a) Decreased motor activity
    (b) Spasm of extermities
    (c) Both of the above
    (d) None of the above.

20. **Osteporosis is associated with**
    (a) Defective osteoclasts
    (b) Loss of bone mass

(c) Deficient mineral acreation

(d) Oestrogen administration.

21. **Calcium metabolism is affected by the following hormones except**

(a) Parathormone

(b) Glucocorticoids

(c) Insulin

(d) Catecholamines.

22. **Calcitonin has one of the following actions**

(a) Inhibition of osteoclast formation

(b) Inhibition of osteoclastic

(c) Osteroporotic action

(d) Increasing Ca^{2+} absorption from the intestine.

23. **The following are the action of 1,25 dihydroxy cholecalciferol except**

(a) Mobilization of Ca^{2+} and PO_4^{3-} from bone

(b) Facilitation of Ca^{2+} reabsorption in the kidney

(c) Increasing the urinary Ca^{2+} levels

(d) Increased absorption of Ca^{2+} from the intestine.

24. **Ca^{2+} excretion in the urine is facilitated by the following hormones except**

(a) Calcitonin

(b) Growth hormone

(c) 1, 25 dihydroxy cholecalciferol

(d) Glucocorticoids.

26. **Carpopedal spasm can be precipitated by**

(a) O_2 administration

(b) Voluntary hyperventilation

(c) Muscular exercise

(d) Ingestion of ammonium chloride.

27. The endocrine pancreas exhibits the following features

   (a) Reglilation of intestinal glandular secretion

   (b) Paracrine mode of secretion

   (c) Secretion of steroid hormones

   (d) Hypothalamic control.

28. Insulin causes the following effects

   (a) Inhibition of gluconeogenesis

   (b) Glucose entry into muscle

   (c) Both of the above

   (d) None of the above.

29. Diabetes mellitus is charactrized by

   (a) Deficient glucose utlization

   (b) Protein catabolism

   (c) Both of the above

   (d) None of the above.

30. Insulin release is facilitated by

   (a) Decrease in plasma glucose

   (b) Adrenaline

   (c) Somatostatin

   (d) Glucagon.

31. The inhibitors of insulin secretion include the following except

   (a) Somatostatin

   (b) Norepinephrine

   (c) Acetyl choline

   (d) Beta blockers.

32. Insulin facilitates glucose uptake in the following tissues except

   (a) Skeletal muscles

   (b) Cerebral cortex

(c) Adipose tissue

(d) Pituitary.

33. **Protein anabolic hormones include the following except**

(a) Insulin

(b) Growth hormones

(c) Androgens

(d) Glucocorticoids.

34. **Insulin secretion is decreased by**

(a) Glucagon

(b) Orally administered amino acids

(c) K^+ depletion

(d) β-adrenergic sitmulators.

35. **Uncontrolled diabetes exhibits one of the following features**

(a) Alkalosis

(b) Lipemic plasma

(c) Positive nitrogen balance

(d) Obesity.

36. **Hyperphagia in diabetes mellitus is due to**

(a) Increased fat catabolism

(b) Glycogen depletion

(c) Decreased activity of the hypothalmic satiety centre

(d) Glycosuria.

37. **The Na^+ glucose cotransporter present in small intestine and renal tubules is**

(a) GLUT-1

(b) Na^+ H^+ - ATPase

(c) SGLT -1

(d) H^+ K^+ -ATPase.

38. **In the adipose tissue, insulin causes**

(a) Decreased K^+ uptake

(b) Increased fatty acid synthesis

(c) Increased ketognesis

(d) Inhibition of lipoprotein lipase.

39. **The action of glucocorticoids on the intermediary metabolism includes**

(a) Protein catabolism

(b) Hepatic glycogenesis

(c) Both of the above

(d) None of the above.

40. **The role of glucocorticoids in resisting stress includes the following**

(a) Movement of fluid into the vascular system

(b) Deposition of fat in adipose tissue

(c) Dilation of capillaries

(d) Hepatic lipogenesis.

41. **The actions of aldosterone include**

(a) Increased Na^+ reabsorption from gastric juice

(b) Decrease in urine acidity

(c) Rise in plasma K^+

(d) Reduction of plasma volume.

42. **Adrenal insufficiency exhibits the following features**

(a) Severe K^+ depletion

(b) Muscle weakness

(c) Hypotension

(d) Hypernatremia

43. The following are the features of adrenal insufficiency except

(a) Absence of vascular responses to catecholamines

(b) Hypovolemia

(c) Vasoconstriction

(d) Inability to excrete water.

44. Glucocorticoids causes

(a) Eosinophilia

(b) Lymphopenia

(c) Basophilia

(d) Anaemia.

45. The anti-inflammatory effects of cortisol include the following except

(a) Lysosome stabilization

(b) Inhibition of antigen-antibody reaction

(c) Suppression of T cells

(d) Inhibition of fibroblastic activity.

46. Na^+ excretion is increased by the following except

(a) Atrial natriuretic peptide

(b) Hypoaldosteronism

(c) Increased glomerular filtration rate

(d) Haemorrhage.

47. Cushing's syndrome is characterized by the following except

(a) Protein depletion

(b) Abdominal state

(c) Poor wound healing

(d) Increased osteogenesis.

48. **Adrenogenital syndrome is characterized by**

(a) Female pseudohermophroditism

(b) Decreased ACTH

(c) True hermophroditism

(d) None of the above.

49. **The main regulator of aldosterone secretion is**

(a) Plasma Na^+ level

(b) Plasma K^+ level

(c) Circardian rhythm

(d) Hypothalamus.

50. **Aldosterone secretion is increased by**

(a) High potassium intake

(b) Surgery

(c) Haemorrhage

(d) High sodium intake.

51. **The action of nor epinephrine include**

(a) Decrease in peripheral resistance

(b) Increase in cardiac output

(c) Widening of pulse pressure

(d) Elevation of mean arterial pressure.

52. **The metabolic effects of catecholamines include all except**

(a) Fat depostion

(b) Glycogenolysis in liver and skeletal muscle

(c) Rise in metabolic rate

(d) Activation of phosphorylase.

53. **Stimulation of beta 2 adrenergic receptor causes**

(a) Pilo motor contraction

(b) Coronory vasodilation

(c) Pulmonary vasoconstriction

(d) Mydriasis

54. The following events takes place during the fear reaction

(a) Fall in arterial blood pressure

(b) Increased visceral blood flow

(c) Fall in blood glucose level

(d) Diversion of blood flow to brain and heart.

55. The effects of dopamine include all except

(a) Renal vasodilation

(b) Positive ionotroptism

(c) Increase in diastolic pressure

(d) Increase in systolic pressure.

56. Stimulation of alpha adrenergic receptors causes

(a) Vasoconstriction

(b) Bronchodilation

(c) Cardio accleration

(d) Lipolysis.

57. Epinephrine causes

(a) Bradycardia

(b) Renal vasodilation

(c) Vasodilation in skeletal muscle

(d) Rise in systolic and diastolic blood pressure.

58. Conversion of epinephrine to metanephrine is accomplished by

(a) Monoamine oxidase

(b) Phenylethanol amine-N- methyl transferase

(c) Catechol-O- methyl transferase

(d) Dopa carboxylase.

59. **Administration of nor epinephrine to an isolated heart preparation can cause**

(a) Decrease in the force of contraction

(b) Increase in the rate of contraction

(c) Decrease in myocardial excitability

(d) Coronary vasodilation.

60. **Growth hormone exerts all of the following effects except**

(a) Decrease in circulationg free fatty acids

(b) Diabetogenesis

(c) Increase in visceral size

(d) Decrease in body fat content.

61. **Somatomedins are associated with all features except**

(a) Incorporation of sulphate into cartilage

(b) Insulin

(c) Protein metabolism

(d) Elevating plasma FFA levels.

62. **Growth is acclerated by**

(a) Growth hormone

(b) Androgens

(c) Both of the above

(d) None of the above.

63. **The pubertal growth spurt is associated with**

(a) Insulin secretion

(b) Cyclical changes in LHRH release

(c) Increase IGF-1

(d) None of the above.

64. **Pituitary hyperfunction in an adult causes**

(a) Acromegaly

(b) Decreased body hair

(c) Poor cold tolerance

(d) Disappearance of secondary sexual characters.

65. Growth failure in a young boy is due to

(a) Adrenocortical insufficiency

(b) Diabetes mellitus

(c) Hyperthyroidism

(d) Hyperpituitarism.

66. Pituitary insufficiency causes the following effects except

(a) Salt loss and hypovolemia

(b) Extreme sensitivity to stress

(c) Growth inhibition

(d) Gonadal atrophy.

67. Hyperpigmentation is a sign of

(a) Hypopituitarism

(b) Primary adrenal insufficiency

(c) Adrenal insufficiency secondary to pituitary disease

(d) Vitiligo.

68. The secretion of growth hormone is increased by the following stimuli except

(a) Exercise

(b) Fasting

(c) Cortisol

(d) Protein meal.

69. Hypophysectomy in an adult can cause

(a) Absence of secondary sexual characteristics

(b) Sterility in the female

(c) Insulin resistance

(d) Gross skeletal changes.

70. **Growth hormone is known to cause**
    (a) Increase in fat content of body
    (b) Insulin like activity
    (c) Incorporation of sulfate into cartilage
    (d) Accleration of chondrogenesis.

71. **Vasopressin causes the following effects except**
    (a) Decrease in the collecting duct permeability
    (b) Increase of urine osmolality
    (c) Water retention
    (d) Fall in body fluid osmolality.

72. **Vasopressin secretion is increased by the following stimuli except**
    (a) Haemorrhage
    (b) Dehydration
    (c) Burns
    (d) Water retention.

73. **Oxytocin has the following effects**
    (a) Powerful constriction of the arterioles
    (b) Contraction of the parturent uterus
    (c) Powerful natriuretic action
    (d) Diuretic action.

74. **Water toxicity causes**
    (a) Rise in ADH secretion
    (b) Increased renal absorption of water
    (c) Stimulation of concentrated urine
    (d) Decresed permeability of collecting duct.

75. **Positive feedback operates in the case of following except**
    (a) Milk ejection reflex
    (b) Pre-ovulatory LH surge

(c) Parturition

(d) Menstruation.

76. **Oxytocin is known to cause**

   (a) Contraction of the skeletal muscle

   (b) Secretion of milk

   (c) Contraction of uterine smooth muscle

   (d) Maturation of sperms.

77. **Vasopressin acts by**

   (a) Enhancing Na^+ reabsorption in the proximal tubule

   (b) Increasing the permeability of collecting ducts to H_2O.

   (c) Increasing water reabsorption in the proximal tubule

   (d) Enhancing counter current exchange.

78. **The biological actions of prostaglandin $F_2\alpha$ include the following except**

   (a) Inhibition of sodium and water reabsorption

   (b) Painful uterine contractions

   (c) Platelet aggragation

   (d) Contraction of bronchiolar smooth muscle.

79. **Pinealectomy in experimental mammals causes**

   (a) Decrease in ovarian weight

   (b) Induction of ovulation

   (c) Decreaed secretion of female and male sex hormones

   (d) Decrease in thyroid hormone secretion.

80. **Prostaglandins of the E series are known to cause**

   (a) Increased slow wave sleep

   (b) Inhibition of gastric acid secretion

   (c) Platelet aggregation

   (d) Constriciton of ductus areriosus.

81. The posterior lobe of pituitary is

(a) Glandular

(b) Neural

(c) Ganlionic

(d) Vascular.

82. The hormones of the posterior pituitary are oxytocin and vasopressin but the latter is better known are

(a) Antidiuretic hormone

(b) Growth hormone

(c) Corticotrophic

(d) Neurohypophyseal.

83. The hormone that acts during parturition but which has more effect on lactation is

(a) Progestin

(b) Prolactin

(c) Oxytocin

(d) Vasopressin.

84. The other name for anterior pituitary is

(a) Neurohypophysis

(b) Pars tuberalis

(c) Pars intermedia

(d) Adenohypophysis.

85. The growth of the corpus luteum is initiated by

(a) Follicle stimulating hormone (FSH)

(b) Interstitial cell stimulating hormone (ICSH)

(c) Gonadotrophic hormone

(d) Luteotrophic hormone.

86. **The hormone that maintains the secretory activity of corpus luteum as well as increase in the size of the mammary gland is**

    (a) Oestrogen

    (b) Leutenizing

    (c) Luteotropin

    (d) Gonadotrophin.

87. **The hormones that have influences on other endocrine glands of the body such as thyroid, gonad, etc. are secreted by**

    (a) Anterior pituitary

    (b) Posterior pituitary

    (c) Pars Intermedia

    (d) Pars tuberalis.

88. **The nervous control of pituitary secretion lies in**

    (a) Infundibulum

    (b) Pituitary centre

    (c) Hypothalamus

    (d) Medulla oblongata.

89. **Hyperpituitarism in the adult cause a disease called**

    (a) Gigantism

    (b) Acromegaly

    (c) Cushing syndrome

    (d) Addison's disease.

90. **The adrenal cortical hormone that reduces inflammation and produce healing response is**

    (a) Corticosterone

    (b) Deoxy corticosterone

    (c) Cortisone

    (d) Aldosterone

91. The mineralocorticoid of the adrenal cortex hormone which causes Na²⁺ retention and K⁺ excretion is

(a) Cortisol

(b) Corticosterone

(c) Progesterone

(d) Aldosterone.

92. The disease characterized by extreme muscular weakness and brownish pigmentation of buccal caity and skin is

(a) Cushing's syndrome

(b) Addision's diséase

(c) Grave's disease

(d) Myxoedema.

93. Cushing syndrome which is characterized by wasting of limb muscles and accumulation of fat in the trunk region is due to hypersecretion of

(a) Corticosteroids

(b) Adrenaline

(c) Progesterone

(d) Adrenocorticotrophin.

94. When an animal is angry and it wants to fight, the hormone that is secreted is

(a) Adrenalin

(b) Androgen

(c) Corticosterone

(d) Glucocorticoids.

95. The thyroid gland, for proper secretion requires enough of

(a) Iodine

(b) Thyroxine

(c) Iron

(d) Copper.

96. **Hypothyrodism in adults causes**

(a) Cretinsm

(b) Grave's disease

(c) Myxoedema

(d) Exophthalmic goitre.

97. **Cretinism in children is caused by**

(a) Hypothyroidism

(b) Hyperpituitarism

(c) Hypoparathyroidism

(d) Hypo-insulin-secretion.

98. **The basal metabolic rate is increased due to over secretion of**

(a) Parathormone

(b) Cortisone

(c) Somatotrophin

(d) Thyroxine.

99. **The secondary sexual characters in male are maintained by**

(a) Oestrogen

(b) Progesterone

(c) Testosterone

(d) Growth hormone.

100. **Calcium and phosphate metabolism is controlled by**

(a) Thyroxine

(b) Parathormone

(c) Aldosterone

(d) Cortisol.

101. Hypoparathyroidism results in

    (a) Upset in metabolism

    (b) Improper gonadial funciton

    (c) Convulsions and tetany

    (d) Nervousness and wasting.

102. Histamine is a hormone released by the tissues of the body, it causes

    (a) Itching and pain

    (b) Inhibition of clotting

    (c) Increase in blood pressure

    (d) Reduced secretion by glands.

103. The endocrine gland that slowly atrophies during puberty is

    (a) Parathyroid

    (b) Pineal

    (c) Thymus

    (d) Corpus luteum.

104. The a cells of pancreas secrete a hormone called glucagon which

    (a) Reduces pancreatic secretion

    (b) Stimulates pancreatic secretion

    (c) Increases blood sugar level

    (d) Reduces blood sugar level.

105. Diabetes mellitus is caused by the hyposecretion of

    (a) Glucagon

    (b) Insulin

    (c) Secretin

    (d) Vasopressin.

106. Insulin was extracted first by

(a) Fleming

(b) Kluorana

(c) Watson and Crick

(d) Banting and Best.

107. Islets of langerhans which secrete insulin are found in

(a) Stomach

(b) Liver

(c) Spleen

(d) Pancreas.

108. The hormone progestrone is secreted by

(a) Graffian follicle

(b) Corpus luteum

(c) Anterior pituitary

(d) Testes.

109. The thickening of the endometrium of the uterus for the implantation of the ovum is due to the secretion of

(a) Corpus luteum

(b) Adrenal cortex

(c) Graffian follicle

(d) Anterior pituitary.

110. During pregnancy, ovulation does not take place becuase of the inhibitory action of

(a) Progesterone

(b) Gonadotrophin

(c) Androgen

(d) Oestrogen.

111. **The hormone that helps in the relaxation of pelvis during parturition is**

    (a) Progesterone

    (b) Oestrogen

    (c) Luteinizing hormone

    (d) Oxytocin.

112. **The ovulation is largely due to action of**

    (a) Luteinizing hormone

    (b) Follicle stimulating hormone

    (c) Luteotrophin

    (d) Progesterone.

113. **The initation of milk secretion is due to the hormone prolactin otherwise called**

    (a) Luteotrophin

    (b) Oestrogen

    (c) Estradiol

    (d) Oxytocin.

Answer sheet is at the end of the book.

Chapter 13

REPRODUCTIVE SYSTEM

1. **In the case of mammals testes are found in scrotal sacs outside the viscera because**
    (a) Mammals are highly evolved animals
    (b) Sperms require a lower temperature
    (c) Of the presence of long vas deferens
    (d) Of the presence of urinary bladder.

2. **There is a connective tissue cord extending between the testis and abdominal wall called**
    (a) Testis cord
    (b) Gubernaculum
    (c) Mesentric cord
    (d) Spermatic cord.

3. **The elastic tissue connecting the cauda epididymis to the scrotal sac is**
    (a) Gubernaculum
    (b) Tendinous cord
    (c) Scrotal ligament
    (d) Caput epididymus.

4. **The seminiferous tubules of the testis are lined by the germinal epithelium consisting of**
    (a) Cells of sertoli
    (b) Spermatocyte
    (c) Spermatogonia
    (d) Spermatids.

5. **Between the spermatagonia are the**

    (a) Epithetial cells

    (b) Cells of sertoli

    (c) Lymph spaces

    (d) Capillaries.

6. **The sperms achieve motility and maturity in**

    (a) Prostate gland

    (b) Epididymis

    (c) Seminal vesicle

    (d) Cowper's gland.

7. **The hormone testosterone is secreted by**

    (a) Interstitial cells

    (b) Germinal epithelium

    (c) Rete testis

    (d) Seminiferous tubule.

8. **Inguinal canal is the connection between the scrotal sac and the**

    (a) Tunica vaginalis

    (b) Urethral lumen

    (c) Abdominal cavity

    (d) Uterus masculinus.

9. **The layers of cells immediately surrounding the ovum but outside the zona pellucida is called**

    (a) Corona radiata

    (b) Membrana granulosa

    (c) Theca interna

    (d) Germinal epithelium.

10. **The membrane investing the ovum just outside the membrana granulosa is**

   (a) Zona pellcida

   (b) Theca interna

   (c) Vitelline membrane

   (d) Discus proligerus.

11. **After ovulation the Graffian follice becomes an endocrine organ called**

   (a) Interstitial organ

   (b) Ovarian tube

   (c) Placenta

   (d) Corpus luteum.

12. **The stroma of the ovary consists of nerves, blood vessels, muscles fibres and a type of protein called**

   (a) Collagen

   (b) Albumin

   (c) Globulin

   (d) Fibrin.

13. **Because of the uniform distribution of small amount of yolk, the eggs are known as**

   (a) Megalecthal

   (b) Telolecithal

   (c) Centrolecithal

   (d) Microlecithal.

14. **The acrosome of the sperm contain**
   (a) Sugars

   (b) Enzymes

   (c) Cytoplasm

   (d) Nucleus.

15. The cytoplasmic part of the sperm cell is the

(a) Head

(b) Neck

(c) Tail

(d) Axis.

16. Fertilization takes place in

(a) Vagina

(b) Uterus

(c) Cervix

(d) Fallopian tube

17. The nutritive medium for the ejaculated sperms is given by the

(a) Seminal fluid

(b) Vaginal fluid

(c) Uterine lining

(d) Fallopian tube.

18. The embryonic membrane that forms the placenta is called the

(a) Allontois

(b) Chorion

(c) Amnion

(d) Umbilicus.

19. The layer of uterus which becomes much eroded due to placental villi is known as

(a) Endothelium

(b) Endometrium

(c) Endoderm

(d) Trophoblast.

20. Placenta has an outer layer which is selectively permeable and hormone secreting which is known as

(a) Trophoblast

(b) Chorion

(c) Amnion

(d) Mesoderm

21. In amniotes such as mammals the amnion serves the embryo for

(a) Excretion

(b) Development

(c) Protection

(d) Absorption.

22. The cells of the testes which produce testosterone are

(a) Sertoli cells

(b) Leydig cells

(c) Spermatogonia

(d) Germinal epithelium.

23. The cells of the interstitial compartment of the testis

(a) Are unable to function unless the testis descends into scrotum

(b) Are not influenced by the neurosecretory cells of hypothalamus

(c) Secrete seminal fluid

(d) Are stimulated by LH of anterior pituitary.

24. Testosterone causes

(a) Sperms to become motile

(b) An increase in scalp hair

(c) A negative nitrogen balance

(d) The epiphysis of long bones to unite.

25. Androgens
   (a) Are formed in greater quantity in foetal life than in childhood
   (b) Are secreted in small quantities in adult females
   (c) Have anabolic effect
   (d) All of the above.

26. Spermatozoa
   (a) Are normally stored in the epididymis at a temperature below that of body core
   (b) When separated from the other constituents of semen are infertile
   (c) Require FSH for spermatogenesis
   (d) All of the above.

27. Human spermatozoa
   (a) Are motile in seminiferous tubules
   (b) Are mostly bifid
   (c) Contains 23 chromosomes
   (d) Are produced at a faster rate when testicular.

28. The normal seminal fluid
   (a) Has an average volume of 2-5 ml/ ejaculate
   (b) Has an average number of 80-200 million sperms/ ml
   (c) Coagulates once it is ejaculated
   (d) All of the above.

29. Erection in male
   (a) Can occur in a patient whose spinal cord has been severed in the lower thoracic region
   (b) Does not occur during infancy
   (c) Is essential for ejaculation
   (d) Is initated by the constriciton action of noradrenaline of the veins draining the erectile tissues.

30. Ejaculation of semen

(a) Involves rhythmic contractions of striated muscles.

(b) Is aided by sympathetic nerve activity

(c) Coincides with feeling of orgasm

(d) All of the above.

31. Which of the following statement is incorrect? Human spermatozoa normally

(a) Contain 23 chromosomes

(b) Contain either X or Y chromosomes but not both

(c) Can survive in the female genital tract for 1 and 2 days or longer

(d) Are produced at an accelerated rate when testicular temperature is raised from 35^0 C to 37^0 C.

32. Undescended testis

(a) Is associated with faiture to produce testosterone

(b) Does not interfere with fertility

(c) Should be treated by injection of testosterone

(d) Makes it more prone to malignant change.

33. A child with sex chromosome pattern of

(a) XX develops into a normal female

(b) XXY develops into a true hermophrodite

(c) XO shows incomplete sexual maturation at puberty

(d) XXX develops excessive female secondary characters.

34. Follicle stimulating hormone

(a) Helps in maturation and growth of follicles

(b) Facilitates spermatogenesis

(c) Release is under control of hypothalmic factor

(d) All of the above.

35. **After 6 months of castration an adult would have**

   (a) Atrophy of prostate gland

   (b) A decrease in secretion of LH

   (c) Abolition of sex drive or libido

   (d) An increased pitch of voice.

36. **In the adult human subject, prolactin**

   (a) Facilitates development of Leydig cells of the testes

   (b) Facilitates release of FSH

   (c) Facilitates secretory activity of corpus luteum

   (d) In the presence of ovarian and adrenal cortical hormones, promotes growth and development of breasts.

37. **Puberty does not occur if**

   (a) Castration has been done in childhood

   (b) Hypophysectomy has been done in childhood

   (c) Either castration or hypophysectomy done in childhood

   (d) Uterus has been removed in girl.

38. **The ovaries**

   (a) Start to produce ova at puberty

   (b) Go on producing ova throughout life

   (c) Discharge 5-10 ova during each menstrual cycle

   (d) All of the above.

39. **As compared to 7th day, on 21st day of menstrual cycle there is greater**

   (a) Progesterone level in blood

   (b) Secretory activity of the endometrium

   (c) Body temperature

   (d) All of the above.

40. In the normal menstrual cycle

    (a) On an average, female loses about 40 ml of blood during menstruation

    (b) Ovulation is associated with a sudden rise in LH levels in blood

    (c) Proliferative phase of endometrium depends on oestrogen

    (d) All of the above.

41. In the days following ovulation

    (a) The body temperature rises

    (b) The plasma progesterone level rises

    (c) The plasma level of LH falls

    (d) All of the above.

42. Fertilization of the ovum usually occurs

    (a) In the uterus

    (b) In the uterus upto 5 days after ovulation

    (c) Upto 5 days after ovulation

    (d) 6 days before implantation

43. Menstruation in a normal healthy and young woman

    (a) Is a period of secretion of endometrium of the uterus

    (b) Occurs at middle of the cycle 1 or 2 days after ovulation

    (c) Occurs 1 to 2 days after the formation of a corpus albicans in the ovary

    (d) Occur several hours after the formation of corpus luteum in the ovary.

44. **Which of the following hormones is responsible for controlling the secretory phase of endometrium**

(a) LH

(b) Prolactin

(c) Oestrogen

(d) Progesterone.

45. **LH of anterior pituitary is**

(a) Essential for maturation and development of corpus luteum

(b) Essential for ovulation

(c) Inhibited by rising levels of progesterone

(d) All of the above.

46. **The effect of maternal chorionic gonadotrophin on the foetal testis is similar to that of**

(a) FSH

(b) ICSH

(c) Testosterone

(d) Luteotropic hormone.

47. **Which of the following secretion is maximum during first trimester of preqnancy**

(a) Oestrogen

(b) Pregnanediol

(c) Chorionic gonadotropin

(d) Oxytocin.

48. **Urinary 17-ketosteroids**

(a) Are not found in women

(b) Reflect the total production of androgenic substances

(c) Include testosterone itself

(d) Are hightly active androgens.

49. **All of the following hormones are produced by placenta except**

(a) HCG

(b) HPL

(c) Oestrogen

(d) Oxytocin.

50. **During pregnant state**

(a) Uterine contractions are absent until 36th week of preganancy

(b) The breast enlarge due to release of prolactin from anterior pituitary

(c) The oxygen tension in the umbilical artery exceeds that in umbilical vein

(d) None of the above is true.

51. **During the last day of pregnancy**

(a) Oxytocin from posterior pitutary is released which decreases the frequency of uterine contractions

(b) Stretching of cervix is a potent stimulus for oxytocin release

(c) Progesterone facilitates uterine contraction

(d) Prostaglandin formation in the decidua of uterus is depressed.

52. **All the following changes in maternal physiology are seen during pregnancy except**

(a) There is a rise in renal threshold for glucose

(b) There is relaxation of smooth muscles in the alimentary tract and uterus

(c) Blood volume rises

(d) There is positive nitrogen balance.

53. In the new born

(a) There is little resistance to infection

(b) The brain cells are less tolerant to lack of oxygen than in the adult

(c) There are no anitbodies circulating in the blood

(d) The biliribin level in the blood tends to be highest in the adult.

54. Foetal haemoglobin

(a) Has twise the iron content of adult haemoglobin

(b) Is the only type of haemoglobin that can be identified in foetal life

(c) Forms the major fraction of total haemoglobin for the first year of life

(d) None of the above.

55. Which one of the following statement is incorrect

(a) The first primary teeth appear at about 6 months

(b) There are a total of 32 primary teeth

(c) There are a total of 32 permanent teeth

(d) All of the above.

56. Puberty before the age of 10 years

(a) May be caused by destruction of pituitary

(b) Causes a delay in the closure of epiphyseal plates

(c) In over 80% cases is caused by pathology

(d) None of the above.

57. In a lactating woman

(a) Oxytocin is essential for milk secretion

(b) Nursing inhibits the secretion of FSH and LH

(c) Prolactin causes secretion of milk

(d) All of the above.

58. Currently available methods of reducing fertility includes

(a) Depression of spermatogenesis by inhibition of FSH release

(b) Confining coitus to 10th-20th day of the cycle

(c) The use of agents which prevent implantation of fertilized ovum

(d) Agents which inhibit release of releasing factors from hypothalamus.

59. Infertility is usually

(a) Seen when sperm count in the ejaculate is less than 10 million/ml

(b) Due to a disorder of endocrine function in both male and female partner

(c) Present when there is loss of function of posterior pituitary in females

(d) Due to a defect of function in female partner than the male.

60. Secondary amenorrhoea

(a) May be due to psychological disturbances

(b) May occur in adrenal hyperplasia

(c) May be caused by continuous administration of oestrogen and progesterone

(d) May occur in all of the above states.

61. Puberty does not occur in

(a) Children who are dwarf

(b) Girls who are blind

(c) Children who have been castrated

(d) Children suffering from malnutrition.

62. Deficiency of testosterone results

(a) In a reduction of male fertility

(b) In raising LH levels in blood

(c) In a paler complexion

(d) In all of the above.

63. A diagnosis of foetal distress can be made if

(a) There is substained increase in foetal heart rate

(b) Meconium is present in the amniotic fluid

(c) Blood sample taken from foetal scalp vein has pH of 7.25

(d) The foetus keeps making vigorous repetitive movements.

64. Foetal death is the typical result of absence of foetal

(a) Brain function

(b) Cardiac function

(c) Kidney function

(d) Liver function.

65. In old male

(a) The secretion of FSH and LH diminshes.

(b) The testes become smaller and spermatogenesis decreases

(c) The proportion of unbound, biologically active testosterone falls

(d) All of the features are seen.

66. Prolactin in males

(a) Is present in plasma in similiar proportion as in females

    (b) Shows increase in its plasma level with advent of puberty

    (c) Decrease on castration

    (d) Shows all the above features.

67. The prostatic fluid is important because

    (a) It increases the acidity of seminal fluid

    (b) It neutralizes the pH of the vaginal secretions

    (c) It contains fructose

    (d) It contains clotting factors.

68. The function of LH in the male is

    (a) Promotion of spermatogenesis

    (b) Stimulation of testosterone secretion

    (c) Promotion of adrenal androgen secretion

    (d) Promotion of sertoli cell development

69. Sperm count can be reduced by

    (a) Cold baths

    (b) Descent of testes into the scrotum

    (c) Athletic tight cloth binders

    (d) Counter current heat exchange between spermatic arteries and veins.

70. Testosterone is associated with

    (a) Negative feedback on pituitary LH

    (b) Protein catabolism

    (c) Descent of testes

    (d) Stimulaiton by HCG.

71. **Eunuchoidism has the following features**
   (a) Leydig cell deficiency from childhood
   (b) Short individuals
   (c) Premature epiphyseal closure
   (d) None of the above.

Answer sheet is at the end of the book.

Chapter 14

NERVOUS SYSTEM

1. The Nissil granules which are associated with the cell body of the neuron, contain
   (a) RNA
   (b) DNA
   (c) Ribosome
   (d) Proteins.

2. The axon contains in its axis cylinder a fibrellar component of 90 Å thick called
   (a) Axial fibrils
   (b) Myofibrils
   (c) Neurofibrils
   (d) Myelin fibrils.

3. The neurilemma surrounds the
   (a) Axis cylinder
   (b) Cell body
   (c) Sheath of Schwann
   (d) Endoneurium.

4. The junctions between Schwann cells are known as
   (a) Plasmalemma
   (b) Nodes of Ranvier
   (c) Dendrons
   (d) Synapses.

5. **Bundles of nerve fibre are enclosed in a sheath called**

    (a) Fascide

    (b) Endoneurium

    (c) Epineurium

    (d) Perineurium.

6. **In a resting nerve these is a mechanism known as 'Sodium Pump' which result in**

    (a) Na^+ being pumped out

    (b) Na^+ being pumped in

    (c) Exchanging Na^+ for K^+

    (d) Na^+ being pumped into the cell.

7. **Conduction of an impulse along an axon is associated with**

    (a) Resting potential

    (b) Cl concentration

    (c) Strength of an impulse

    (d) Action poiential.

8. **The potential difference in the membrane which is responsible for the conduction of an impulse is brought about by a change in the membrane**

    (a) Permeability

    (b) Structure

    (c) Anions

    (d) Concentration.

9. **When an impulse is passing the membrane is depolarised and the outside of the cell is**

    (a) Positive and inside negative

    (b) Inside positive and outside negative

    (c) Both sides have zero potential

    (d) Both sides are electronegative.

10. **The rate of rise of action potential and its amplitude are determined by the concentration of**

   (a) K^+

   (b) Cl^-

   (c) Na^+

   (d) OH^-

11. **The resting potential of the membrane is**

   (a) -60 to -70 mV

   (b) -100 to -110 mV

   (c) 50 to 100 mV

   (d) -20 to -30 mV.

12. **The rate of conduction of impulses in a motor nerve of a mammal is**

   (a) 4 m/sec

   (b) 10 m/sec

   (c) 50 m/sec

   (d) 100 m/sec

13. **The rate of conduction in a myelinated fibre of the mammal is very high because**

   (a) The synapses are less frequent

   (b) Action potentials are faster and numerous

   (c) Action potentials jump from node to node

   (d) Membrane is depolarised faster.

14. **The weakest current strength that can excite a tissue is called the**

   (a) Chronaxie

   (b) Rheobase

   (c) Saltatory

   (d) Reflex arc

15. **The jumping of action potentials form node to node (of ranvier) in a fibre is called**

    (a) All or none principle

    (b) Threshold stimulus

    (c) Nodal conductioin

    (d) Saltatory conduction.

16. **Chronaxie value helps to find the relative excitability of the nerve. Chronaxie is**

    (a) Duration of two rheobases

    (b) Duration of one rheobase

    (c) Threshold stimulus needed

    (d) Current of subthreshold strength.

17. **In the synapses of central nervous system the impulses from one dendrite pass to another dendrite by**

    (a) Continuous depolarization

    (b) Chemical transmitter

    (c) Saltatory conduction

    (d) Change in permeability.

18. **When a constant stimulus is applied, the gradual decrease in the number of impulses in an axon is called**

    (a) Refractory period

    (b) Falling phase

    (c) Repolarisation

    (d) Accomodation.

19. **The region of contact between a motor nerve and a muscle is known as**

    (a) Pre-synoptic membrane

    (b) Terminal dendrons

    (c) Myoneural junction

    (d) Myofibril junction

20. When the axon conveys information about the **strength** of stimulus the action potential becomes

(a) Higher in magnitude

(b) Greater in frequency

(c) Smaller in height

(d) Longer in duration.

21. When the action potential is measured, the cell interior records a change potential to the extent of about

(a) 110 mV

(b) 200 mV

(c) 150 mV

(d) 50 mV.

22. Two thirds of the mammalian brain is made up of

(a) Cerebrum

(b) Cerebellum

(c) Mid brain

(d) Hind brain.

23. The frontal and temporal lobes of the cerebrum are separated by

(a) Median fissure

(b) Rhinal fissure

(c) Sylvian fissure

(d) Hippocampal lobe.

24. The transverse bridge of white matter in cerebrum, characteristic of mammals is called

(a) Crura cerebri

(b) Corpus callosum

(c) Pons varoli

(d) Corpus albicans

25. **Superficial layer of cerbrum which is extensive only in mammals is known as**

(a) Grey matter

(b) White matter

(c) Cerebral cortex

(d) Pia mater.

26. **When a man feels thirty the region that is stimulated is**

(a) Cerebral cortex

(b) Olfactory lobe

(c) Hypothalamus

(d) Cerebellum.

27. **The midbrain contains on the ventral side longitudinal bands of nerve fibres called**

(a) Corpora quadrigemia

(b) Optic thalami

(c) Hypothalamus

(d) Crura cerebri.

28. **The coordination of motor funcitons is brought about by**

(a) Medulla

(b) Cerebrum

(c) Cerebellum

(d) Hypothalamus.

29. **The pons varoli is present in the**

(a) Fore brain

(b) Hind brain

(c) Mid brain

(d) Ventricles.

30. **The connection between the lateral ventricles and the 3rd ventricles of the diencephalon is known as**

   (a) Foramen of Monro

   (b) Foramen of magendie

   (c) Aqueductus sylvius

   (d) 2nd ventricle.

31. **The connection between 3rd and 4th ventricles is known as**

   (a) Foramen

   (b) Plexus

   (c) Iber

   (d) Optocoel.

32. **The cerebrospinal fluid inside and outside the brain is in communication through foramen of Magendie present in the**

   (a) Lateral ventricles

   (b) Posterior choroid plexus

   (c) Anterior choroid plexus

   (d) Aqueductus sylvius.

33. **The vascular membrane above the brain is called**

   (a) Pia matter

   (b) Dura matter

   (c) Arachnoid layer

   (d) Grey matter.

34. **The vestige of the third eye present in the brain is the**

   (a) Corpus albicans

   (b) Infundibulum

   (c) Optic chiasma

   (d) Pineal body.

35. **The human brain weighs about**

    (a) 2 lbs

    (b) 1.5 lbs

    (c) 4 lbs

    (d) 3 lbs.

36. **The brain capacity of man is about**

    (a) 1000 cc

    (b) 2000 cc

    (c) 1500 cc

    (d) 1050 cc.

37. **When the heart is removed from the body and suspended in a suitable medium, it shows spontaneous rhythmic activity which shows that it is controlled by**

    (a) Central nervous system

    (b) Peripheral nervous system

    (c) Autonomic nervous system

    (d) Spinal nervous system.

38. **Afferent nerve proceeding from the visceral organ lies in the**

    (a) Dorsal root ganglion

    (b) Ventral root ganglion

    (c) Cerebral hemispheres

    (d) Meissner's plexus.

39. **The parasympathetic system leaves the central nervous system in the**

    (a) Thoracic and lumbar regions

    (b) Cranial and sacral regions

    (c) Coeliac and mesentric reions

    (d) Cervical and cranial regions.

40. Post ganglionic fibre in parasympathetic system is short because the ganglion lies

(a) Near the spinal cord

(b) Near the organ supplied

(c) In the dorsal root

(d) In the grey matter.

41. The neurohormone secreted by the parasympathetic nerve endings is

(a) Adrenaline

(b) Nor adrenaline

(c) Sympathin

(d) Acetylcholine

42. While many of the organs are depressed in their functioning by acetyl choline it also stimulates organ such as

(a) Heart

(b) Lung

(c) Stomach

(d) Blood vessel

43. The parasympathetic nervous system is associated with cranial nerves

(a) 3, 7, 9, 10

(b) 1, 2, 4, 5

(c) 7, 10, 11, 12

(d) 5, 7, 8, 10.

44. Stimulation of the vagus nerve will make the heart beat

(a) Faster

(b) 70 times/min

(c) Slower

(d) Normal.

45. **The sympathetic nervous system is otherwise called**

  (a) Visceral system

  (b) Mesenteric system

  (c) Thoraco lumbar system

  (d) Cervico-sacral system

46. **The preganglionic fibers to the sympathetic system are short because the ganglion lies near the**

  (a) Brain

  (b) Verterbra

  (c) Thorax

  (d) Spinal nerve.

47. **Vasoconstriction occurs when the sympathetic nerve is stimulated because the neurohormones secreted at the nerve endings is largely**

  (a) Adrenaline

  (b) Nor adrenaline

  (c) Acetlycholine

  (d) Vasopressin.

48. **The similarity between both the sympathetic and parasympathetic system is that - in both post ganglionic fibres are**

  (a) Not myelinated

  (b) Myelinated

  (c) Longer

  (d) Shorter.

49. **The Meissner's and Averbach's plexusl and the almentary canal are connected with**

  (a) Sympathetic system
  (b) Parasympathetic system
  (c) Spinal nerves
  (d) Peripheral nerves.

50. **The nerves arising from the grey matter of the spinal cord and reaching the subvertebral ganglion of the sympathetic chain are called the**

(a) Post ganglionic fibres

(b) Splanchnic nerves

(c) Somatic nerves

(d) Motor nerves.

51. **The membrances of the brain are called**

(a) Peritoneum

(b) Synovials

(c) Meninges

(d) Serosa.

52. **The 4th cranial nerve called the trochlear nerve is a somatic motor and supplies a muscle of the eye called**

(a) Inferior oblique

(b) External rectus

(c) Internal rectus

(d) Superior oblique.

53. **The auditory nerve is the cranial nerve of number**

(a) 10

(b) 9

(c) 8

(d) 12.

54. **The cranial nerve associated with the parasympathetic system that supplies the organs of the viscera is**

(a) Facial

(b) Vagus

(c) Abducent

(d) Trigeminial.

55. **The number of cranial nerves in mammals are**

    (a) 10

    (b) 20

    (c) 12

    (d) 13

56. **The ganglion from which the trigeminol nerve arises is called the**

    (a) Vagus ganglion

    (b) Cervical ganglion

    (c) Neuroglia

    (d) Gasserian ganglion

57. **The number of spinal nerves in a man are**

    (a) 31

    (b) 30

    (c) 10

    (d) 37

58. **The 5th to 8th cervical and the first thoracic spinal nerve arises from**

    (a) Cervical ganglia

    (b) Lumbo-sacral plexus

    (c) Solar plexus

    (d) Brachial plexus.

59. **The last two lumbar and first sacral spinal nerves form the**

    (a) Inferior mesentric plexus

    (b) Coeliaco-mesentric plexus

    (c) Lumbo-sacral plexus

    (d) Superior mesentric plexus.

60. The dorsal root ganglion contains

(a) Sensory neurons

(b) Motor neurons

(c) Association neurons

(d) Synapses of neurons.

61. The inner lining of the central canal of the spinal cord is made up of

(a) Ciliated epithelium

(b) Mosaic epithelium

(c) Endothelium

(d) Neural epithelium.

62. The regions of white matter outside the grey matter of the spinal cord are called the

(a) Horns

(b) Septae

(c) Funiculi

(d) Cornua.

63. The shortest cranial nerve is

(a) Trochlear

(b) Auditory

(c) Optic

(d) Abducent.

64. The calcareous glands present at the base of the spinal nerves are

(a) Glands of swammerdans

(b) Thyroid glands

(c) Parathyroid glands

(d) Vertebral glands.

65. **The following are the muscarinic actions of acetylcholine except**

    (a) Decrease in heart rate

    (b) Increased glandular secretion

    (c) Increased intestinal motility

    (d) Stimulation of skeletal muscle motor end place

66. **The nicotinic action of acetylcholine is**

    (a) Neuromuscular transmission

    (b) Increased intestinal motility

    (c) Stimulation of post ganglionic sympathetic neurons in large doses

    (d) Increased glandular secretions.

67. **The role of Ca^{++} in neuromuscular junction is to**

    (a) Cause release of acetylcholine

    (b) Increase membrane permeability to Na^+ & K^+

    (c) Prevent acetylcholine from leaking out

    (d) Enhance acetylcholinesterase activity.

68. **Norepinephrine acts in the following way**

    (a) Enhances intestinal contractions

    (b) Exerts mainly alpha adrenergic actions on the smooth muscle

    (c) Inhibits cardiac contractility

    (d) Constricts the pupil.

69. **The sympathetic fibers to most sweat gland**

    (a) Are adrenergic in nature

    (b) Are nor-adrenergic in nature

    (c) Are cholinergic in nature

    (d) Originate in the spinal cord.

70. The action of epinephrine are among the following

(a) Stimulation of beta receptors

(b) Stimulation of alpha receptors

(c) Synthesis of glycogen

(d) Increase in diastolic blood pressure.

71. Sympathetic stimulation causes the following effect except

(a) Increased arterial pressure

(b) Increased glucose breakdown

(c) Stress response

(d) Increased intestinal motility.

72. The following are the results of parasympathetic stimulation except

(a) Increased secretion of apocrine glands

(b) Bronchiolar constriction

(c) Increased peristalsis and tone of the gut

(d) Decreased heart rate.

73. The synaptic transmitter responsible for post synaptic inhibition is

(a) GABA

(b) Glycine

(c) Glutamate

(d) Substance P.

74. Sympathetic blockade can cause

(a) Increased venous return

(b) Cutaneous vasodilation

(c) Delay in gastric emptying

(d) Dilatation of the pupil.

75. **IPSP is seen in**

(a) Axon

(b) Caridac muscle

(c) Synaptic function

(d) Skeletal muscle.

76. **One among the following is phasic receptor**

(a) Free nerve ending

(b) Muscle spindle

(c) Meissner's corpuscle

(d) Carotid sinus.

77. **Itch sensation is carried by**

(a) Myelinated fibers

(b) A delta nerve fibre

(c) A beta nerve fibre

(d) Type C unmyelinated fibers.

78. **All or none transmission occur in**

(a) Rods and cones

(b) Axon

(c) Pacinian corpuscle

(d) Merkel's disc.

79. **The pain experienced by the amputees in the absent limb is an example of**

(a) Weber-Fechnes law

(b) Muller's doctrine of specific energies

(c) Law of projection

(d) Bell- magendic law

80. pH of CSF is sensed by

   (a) Neurons in hypothalamus

   (b) Receptors on ventral surface of medulla

   (c) Cells in OVLT

   (d) Circumventricular organs.

81. Generator potential in a Pacinian corpuscle can be abolished by

   (a) Removal of connection tissue lamellas

   (b) Applying pressure to the first node of Ranvier

   (c) Applying narcotics to the first node of Ranvier

   (d) Sectioning the sensory nerve.

82. The source of generator potential in a Pacinian corpuscle is the

   (a) First node of Ranvier

   (b) Unmyelinated nerve terminal

   (c) Connective tissue lamella

   (d) Myelinated nerve ending.

83. Warmth is conveyed through

   (a) Type C nerve fibers

   (b) A delta myelinated fibers

   (c) Kraus's end bulbs

   (d) Meissner's corpuscles.

84. An example of non-adapting receptor is the

   (a) Free nerve ending

   (b) Golgi tendon organ

   (c) Pacinian corpuscle

   (d) Meissner's corpuscle.

85. **Lips contain large numbers of**

    (a) Paican corpuscles

    (b) Free nerve endings

    (c) Meissner's corpuscles

    (d) Ruffini's endings.

86. **An example of polysynaptic reflex is the**

    (a) Knee jerk

    (b) Ankle jerk

    (c) Jaw jerk

    (d) Abdominal reflex.

87. **Clonus is caused by**

    (a) Cerebellar lesions

    (b) Increased gamma-efferent discharge

    (c) Inhibitory discharge from the basal ganglia

    (d) Lesions in post central gyrus.

88. **Reciprocal innervation involves**

    (a) Monosynaptic reflex arc

    (b) Post synaptic inhibition

    (c) Golgi tendon organ

    (d) Reverberating circuits.

89. **Section of the motor nerve to a muscle causes**

    (a) Spasticity

    (b) Cog-wheel rigidlity

    (c) Flaccidity

    (d) Clonus

90. **Group lb fibres supply**

    (a) Pain and cold receptors

    (b) Muscle spindle

(c) Temperature receptors

(d) Golgi tendon organ.

91. **The muscle spindle response to phasic events occurs through**

(a) Beta-innervation

(b) Alpha-motor innervation

(c) Dynamic gamma efferents

(d) Static gamma efferents.

92. **Tapping the patellar tendon elicits knee jerk after**

(a) 0.6 -0.9 min.

(b) 19 - 24 min.

(c) 0.5 min.

(d) 2 min.

93. **Hyperactive tendon reflexes are present in**

(a) Anterior horn lesions

(b) Parkinsonism

(c) Spinal animals

(d) Anxious patients.

94. **Reverberating circuits occur in**

(a) Ankle jerk

(b) Withdrawal reflexes

(c) Knee jerk

(d) Triceps jerk.

95. **Tendon jerks are of normal briskness in**

(a) Parkinson's disease

(b) Tabes dorsalis

(c) Lower motor neuron lesion

(d) Paraplegia.

96. Lesions of the post central gyrus cause

(a) Complete loss of sensation

(b) Loss of temperature sensation

(c) Loss of pain sensation

(d) Loss of proprioception and fine touch.

97. Destruction of the spinothalamic tracts leads to

(a) Loss of touch localization

(b) Loss of vibratory sensation

(c) Agnosias

(d) Loss of temporal pattern of tactile stimuli.

98. Lesions in the representational hemisphere of the parietal lobe cause

(a) Loss of language function

(b) Astereognosis

(c) Loss of seqential analysis

(d) Aphasia.

99. Unconscious proprioception is subseried by the

(a) Spinoreticular fibres

(b) Spinocerebellar tracts

(c) Lateral spinothalamic tracts

(d) Spinotectal tract.

100. The following regions are rich in opioid peptides mediating pain relfief except

(a) Dorsal horn of the spinal cord

(b) Raphe nuclei

(c) S_2 in the wall of Sylviam fissure

(d) Periaqueductal grey matter.

101. Blocking of A-beta fibers cause

(a) Loss of deep pain

(b) Loss of warmth sensation

    (c) Loss of discrimination of mechano reception

    (d) Loss of pricking pain.

102. Sleep is produced by

    (a) Lesions in the raphe nuclei

    (b) Release of serotonin in the diencephalon

    (c) Stimulation of the RAS

    (d) Irregular sensory stimuli.

103. Narcolepsy implies

    (a) Sleep-walking

    (b) Premature awakening

    (c) Epileptic fits during sleep

    (d) Excessive daytime sleepiness.

104. Cerebellar lesions in the humans cause

    (a) Hypertonia

    (b) Slurred speech

    (c) Motion sickness

    (d) Tremors during rest.

105. Lesions of the spinal motor neurons cause

    (a) Hyper reflexia

    (b) Enhanced muscular tone

    (c) Spastic paralysis

    (d) Muscle atrophy.

106. Babinski sign is produced by

    (a) Damage to the pyramidal tract

    (b) Cerebellar lesions

    (c) Basal ganglia lesions

    (d) Damage to the pyramidal tract.

107. Cerebellar lesions produce

(a) Ataxic gait

(b) Festinant gait

(c) Waddling gait

(d) None of the above.

108. Lesions of the flocculonodular lobe cause

(a) Hypotonia

(b) Ahinesia

(c) Rigidity

(d) Ataxia.

109. Muscle tone is controlled by

(a) The anterior lobe of the cerebellum

(b) The vermis

(c) The flocculonodular lobe

(d) Fastigial nucleus.

110. The most rapidly conducting pathways are the

(a) Corticospinal tracts

(b) Rubrospinal tracts

(c) Spinocerebellar tracts

(d) Lemniscal system.

111. Degenerative changes in the nigrostriatal tract is characterised by

(a) Poverty of movement

(b) Spasticity

(c) Intention tremor

(d) Loss of vibration sense.

112. Righting reflexes are intergrated in the

(a) Cerebral cortex

(b) Lower medulla

(c) Midbrain

(d) Spinal cordl.

113. A decerebrate animal exhibits one of the following features

(a) Righting reflexes

(b) Flexion of the limbs

(c) Tonic neck reflexes

(d) Kyphosis.

114. The circadian timing system is located in

(a) Ventromedial hypothalamic nucleus

(b) Cerebral cortex

(c) Supra chiasmatic nucleus

(d) Medullary nuclei.

115. The vomiting centre is located in

(a) The hypothalmus

(b) The floor of the fourth ventricle

(c) The pons

(d) The medullary reticular formation.

116. Lesion of the ventromedial hypothalamic mucleus causes

(a) Cessation of eating

(b) Loss of weight

(c) Obesity

(d) Omniphagia.

117. Heat activates

(a) Cutaneous vasoconstriction

(b) Increased respiration

(c) Hunger

(d) Horripilation.

118. The following mechanisms are activated by cold except

(a) Anorexia

(b) Shivering

(c) Hunger

(d) Horripilation.

119. Lesions in the Broca's area causes

(a) Excessive talking

(b) Failure to comprehend spoken words

(c) Non-fluent aphasia

(d) Agnosias.

120. Inability to carry out on request a complex or skilled movenment is known as

(a) Alexia

(b) Apraxia

(c) Astereognosis

(d) Agnosia.

121. Astereognosis is caused by

(a) Lesions in the occipital lobe

(b) Lesions in the representational hemisphere of the parietal lobe

(c) Cerebellar lesions

(d) Lesions of the basal ganglia.

122. Electroshock therapy can cause

    (a) Disruption of long term memory

    (b) Retrograde amnesia

    (c) Loss of conditioned reflexes

    (d) Loss of fine skills.

Answer sheet is at the end of the book.

Chapter 15

SPECIAL SENSES

1. **The chemoreceptors in the body are**
   (a) Proprioceptors
   (b) Meissner's Corpuscles
   (c) Olfactory and taste organ
   (d) Free nerve endings.

2. **The part of the tongue that perceives the bitter taste very well is**
   (a) Tip
   (b) Sides
   (c) Top
   (d) Basal.

3. **The stomach pain impulses are received by receptors known as**
   (a) Proprioceptors
   (b) Exteroceptors
   (c) Free nerve ends
   (d) Chemoreceptors.

4. **The sense organ for touch present in the skin is**
   (a) Free nerve endings
   (b) Pacinian corpuscles
   (c) Meissners corpuscles
   (d) Auerbach's plexus.

5.   The Pacinian Corpuscle present in the skin is for
     (a) Pain
     (b) Presure
     (c) Movement
     (d) Temperature.

6.   The friction between the eyelids and the cornea is
     avoided by the secretions of
     (a) Lacrimal glands
     (b) Conjunctiva and eyelids
     (c) Harderian glands
     (d) Meibomian glands

7.   The continuation of the epidermis over the eye is called
     (a) Cornea
     (b) Conjunctiva
     (c) Eyelid
     (d) Nicitating membrane.

8.   When the eye looks at near objects the lens becomes
     more convex due to the
     (a) Contraction of ciliary muscles
     (b) Relaxation of ciliary muscles
     (c) Contraction of iris muscles
     (d) Relaxation of iris muscles.

9.   The pupil becomes bigger to allow in more light during
     dark by the
     (a) Contraction of radial muscles of the iris
     (b) Relaxation of the radial muscle of the iris
     (c) Contraction of circular muscle of the iris
     (d) Contraction of suspensory ligaments.

10. Aqueous humour is present
     (a) In front of the retina
     (b) In front of cornea
     (c) Behind the conjunctiva
     (d) In front of the lens.

11. **Rods contain visual purple or rhodopsin which when light falls, is**

    (a) Absorbed

    (b) Oxidized

    (c) Bleached

    (d) Changed.

12. **The iodopsin which is in cones is for the perception of**

    (a) Light

    (b) Darkness

    (c) Colour

    (d) Faint light.

13. **In the blind spot where the optic nerve leaves the eye**

    (a) Rods and cones are absent

    (b) Only cones are present

    (c) Only rods are present

    (d) Special neurons are present.

14. **In the yellow spot or fovea the cells that are present are**

    (a) Rods and cones

    (b) Only rods

    (c) Only cones

    (d) Predominantly rods

15. **The pressure is maintained on both sides of the tympanum by**

    (a) Auditory meatus

    (b) Fenestra rotunda

    (c) Middle ear

    (d) Eustachian tube.

16. **The region known as macula lutea is contained in**

    (a) Yellow spot

    (b) Blind spot

    (c) Acoustic spot

    (d) Organ of corti.

17. **The pigments in the rods and cones-rhodopsin and iodopsin are chemically**

    (a) Carotenoids

    (b) Fatty carotenoids

    (c) Polysaccharides

    (d) Protein - carotenoids.

18. **Bipolar nerve cells and ganglion cells are found in the**

    (a) Sclerotica

    (b) Cochlea

    (c) Retina

    (d) Cristae.

19. **Light with longest wavelength is**

    (a) Violet

    (b) Red

    (c) Blue

    (d) Green.

20. **Light with the greatest frequency is**

    (a) Violet

    (b) Blue

    (c) Green

    (d) Yellow.

21. **Electromagnetic waves with wavelength shorter than those of light are**

    (a) X-rays

    (b) Gamma rays

    (c) UV rays

    (d) All of the above.

22. Constriction of pupil

    (a) Is mediated via sympathetic nerves

    (b) Increases the refractory power of the eye

    (c) Increases the depth of focus

    (d) Cannot occur in one eye if light is put on opposite eye.

23. Which of the following records of electrical activity gives a measure of eye movements

    (a) Electroretinogram

    (b) Electroencephalogram

    (c) Electro - oculogram

    (d) Electrocardiogram

24. Most of the refraction that ocurs in the eye occur at

    (a) Anterior surface of cornea

    (b) Posterior surface of cornea

    (c) Anterior surface of the lens

    (d) Posterior surface of the lens.

25. Visual activity in a normal individual

    (a) Is greatest in the fovea under light adapted states.

    (b) Can be determined with landott rings

    (c) In the region of blind spot is 1.0/min of arc

    (d) All of the above.

26. In the refracting system of the eye

    (a) The lens can double the refracting power of the eye during accommodatioin in young adult

    (b) The cornea causes more refraction than of the lens.

    (c) The back and front surface of lens contribute equally during contraction

    (d) None of the above.

27. The rods in the retina.

   (a) Are more dense in the fovea region

   (b) Are rendered insensitive by bright light

   (c) Are more numerous in night shift workers

   (d) Comprise one fifth of the receptors in the fovea.

28. Cones of the retina

   (a) Are confined to the fovea and the area immediately adjacent to it

   (b) Are found in the layer of the retina close to the vitreous humour

   (c) Are more sensitive to yellow green light

   (d) Are uniformly distributed all over retina.

29. Rhodopsin is

   (a) Purple pigment

   (b) Most senstive to violet light

   (c) Regenerated when the eyes are closed

   (d) None of the above.

30. Scoptic vision involves the following except

   (a) Rods

   (b) Appreciation of movement

   (c) Dimlight vision

   (d) Increased sensitivity to blue green light.

31. Physiologic nystagmus is associated with

   (a) Blind individuals

   (b) Vestibulo- ocular reflex

   (c) Visual activity

   (d) Labyrinthine impulses.

32. Nyctalopia involves one among the following

   (a) Double vision

   (b) Hemianopic scotomas

(c) Degeneration of rods and cones

(d) Colour blindness.

33. **In humans the primary visual cortex located in the**

(a) Precentral gyrus

(b) Piriform cortex

(c) Sides of the calcarine fissure

(d) Superior temporal gyrus.

34. **Lesions of arc a 18 in the posterior parietal region causes**

(a) Loss of visual sensibility

(b) Loss of light reflex

(c) Impaired perception of depth and distance

(d) Quadrantic hemianopia.

35. **Homogenous hemianopia may be caused by**

(a) Lesion of the perichiasmal area

(b) Lesion of the optic nerve of the same size

(c) Lesion of the optic tract of the opposite side

(d) Lesion of the optic chiasma.

36. **The bone that is in contact with fenestra ovalis is**

(a) Malleus

(b) Incus

(c) Stapes

(d) Auditory.

37. **The internal ear is a membranous organ called the memranous labyrinth of which the part that is used for balancing is known as**

(a) Sacculus

(b) Utriculus

(c) Cochlea

(d) Vestibule.

38. The acoustic organs called cristae are found in

(a) Semicircular canals

(b) Sacculus

(c) Membranous labyrinth.

(d) Ampullae.

39. The tube leading the sacculus into the cranium is called the

(a) Annulus tympanicus

(b) Ductus endolymphaticus

(c) Scala tympani

(d) Cochlear canal.

40. Cochlea contains organs of cortien which a membrane is stretches called the

(a) Tectorial membrane

(b) Reissner's membrane

(c) Basilar membrane

(d) Sensory epithelium.

41. The part in which the organ of corti are situated is the

(a) Scala media

(b) Scala vestibuli

(c) Scala tympani

(d) Perilymph.

42. The otoliths, the movement of which is registered by the sensory hairs in acoustic spots are present in

(a) Endolymph

(b) Perilymph

(c) Cochlea

(d) Semicircular canals.

43. The semicircular canals are believed to perceive only

    (a) Sideways movement

    (b) Backward movement

    (c) Rotation of the body

    (d) Forward movement

44. The bony labyrinth of ear is filled with a fluid called

    (a) Endolymph

    (b) Synovial fluid

    (c) Perilymph

    (d) Humour

45. The range of human hearing is

    (a) 10,000 to 20,000 cycles/sec

    (b) 1000 to 5000 cycles/sec

    (c) 64 to 2000 cycles/sec

    (d) 30 to 20,000 cycles/sec.

46. The apex of the cochlea responds only to sounds of

    (a) High frequency

    (b) Low frequency

    (c) Medium frequency

    (d) Both low and high frequency.

47. The following are the features of the auditory pathways except

    (a) Contralateral transmission

    (b) Orderliness of projection

    (c) Diversity in the pathways

    (d) Temporal dispersion.

48. **Detection of linear accleration is performed by**

   (a) Crista ampullaris

   (b) Otolithic organ

   (c) Cerebellum

   (d) Lateral semicircular canals.

49. **During nomal hearing conduction of sound waves occur through**

   (a) Air conduction

   (b) Bone conduction

   (c) Ossicular conduction

   (d) Nerve conduction

50. **Orientation in space depends on the following factors except**

   (a) Visual activity

   (b) Vestibular receptors

   (v) Visual cues

   (d) Joint proprioceptors.

51. **In a myopic individual**

   (a) Close vision is more seriously affected than distant vision

   (b) A circular object tends to appear oval

   (c) The eye tends to be larger than average from lens to retina

   (d) Reading becomes difficult without glasses.

52. **Bilateral labyrinthectomy can cause**

   (a) Hypertonia

   (b) Lack of orientation under water

   (c) Flexion of limbs

   (d) Nystagmus.

53. **The first order neurons from the taste receptors synapse in the**

(a) Post central gyrus

(b) Parotid gland

(c) Tongue area of somatic sensory cortex

(d) Nuclei of the tractus solitarius.

54. **Salty taste is produced by**

(a) Dysyltaurine

(b) Lead salts

(c) Acids

(d) Quinine sulphate.

55. **The olfactory receptors project to the**

(a) Limbic lobe

(b) Neocortex

(c) Post central gyrus

(d) Hypothalamus.

56. **Syringing of the right ear with cold air can cause**

(a) Nystagmus with slow component toward the right side

(b) Strabismus

(c) Tendency to fall towards the left side

(d) Interior tremor.

57. **Bilateral labyrinthectomy can cause**

(a) Hypertonia

(b) Lack of orientation under water

(c) Flexion of limbs

(d) Nystagmus

Answer sheet is at the end of the book.

Chapter 16

GENETICS

1. The laws of inheritance were propounded in 1865 by
   (a) Darwin
   (b) G. Mendel
   (c) De vries
   (d) Lamarck.

2. In an dihybrid cross there is a recombinatioin of characters which proves the laws of
   (a) Segregation of characters
   (b) Dominant characters
   (c) Independent assortment
   (d) Recessive characters.

3. The theory of pangenesis was formulated by
   (a) Darwin
   (b) Mendel
   (c) De Vries
   (d) Weismann.

4. Two alleles for black and white from different parents produce in the offspring only black colour. This explains the law of
   (a) Regregation
   (b) Independent assortment
   (c) Dominance
   (d) Incomplete dominance.

5. If an animal or a plant is true breeding i.e. producing the same characters in offsprings also then the animal or plant is said to be

    (a) Heterozygous

    (b) Homozygous

    (c) Allelomorphic

    (d) Dihybrid.

6. In the question above the 3% of recombination can be accounted for by the theory of

    (a) Heterozygosity

    (b) Allelormorphs

    (c) Multiple alleles

    (d) Crossing over.

8. The chromosomes responsible for the determination of sex are called

    (a) Autosomes

    (b) Allosomes

    (c) Multiple alleles

    (d) Heterosis.

9. The theory of recombination of linked genes due to crossing over chromosomes during zygotene of Meiosis was put forward by

    (a) T. H . Morgen

    (b) Punnet

    (c) Mendel

    (d) Conens.

10. If the mother is a carrier for colour blindness and the father is normal in the offsprings this disease may be seen in

(a) All the sons

(b) All the daughters

(c) 50% of sons and 50% daughters

(d) All the sons and not the daughters.

11. The study of Eugenics was started in 1885 by

(a) T.H. Morgan

(b) Garstang

(c) Francis Galton

(d) Freeman

12. Fraternal twins are formed when

(a) A fertilized egg divides into two

(b) An egg is fertitized by two sperms

(c) A divided egg has two sets of chromosomes

(d) Two eggs are fertilized by two sperms.

13. When identical twins formed by the partical reparation of the products of first cleavage remain attached, it is called

(a) Maternal twins

(b) Siamese twins

(c) Fraternal twins

(d) Zygote twins

14. The formation of a male child depends on the sperms because

(a) Sperms may be 'X' or 'Y'

(b) Sperms are all 'Y'

(c) The eggs from the other ovary may by 'Y'

(d) Because sperms are more active.

15. Man's intelligence depends on nature or genotype and narture or environment. These terms nature and nurture were first used by

(a) T.H. Morgan

(b) Muller

(c) Grancis Galton

(d) Freeman.

16. A haemophilic man may survive and reproduce in which case among his offsprings

(a) All sons will be haemophilic

(b) All daughters will be haemophilic

(c) All daughters will be carrier

(d) All the sons will be carriers.

17. The sudden mutations or saltations were first found by

(a) Hugo de Vries

(b) Lamarck

(c) Darwin

(d) Muller.

18. Mutation were first induced in Drosophila by x-rays by

(a) T.H.Morgan

(b) Mullca

(c) Frances Gralton

(d) Landsteiner.

19. Albinism, the absence of skin pigmentation seen occasioinally in man and other animals is due to

(a) Gene mutation

(b) Somatic mutation

(c) Crossing over

(d) Linkage.

20. The appearance of a cancerous tissue and variegated foliage in plant with green leaves are explained in terms of

   (a) Gene mutation

   (b) Somatic mutation

   (c) Environmental effect

   (d) Physiological change.

21. Mutations that are of evolutionary significance are those which are

   (a) Sudden and genotypic

   (b) Continuous and genotypic

   (c) Discontinuous and phenotypic

   (d) Continuous and phenotypic.

22. Mutations are mostly

   (a) Recessive

   (b) Dominant

   (c) Phenotypic

   (d) Discontinuous

23. Sex linked characters are usually

   (a) Nonheritable

   (b) Successive

   (c) Dominant

   (d) Lethal

24. I.Q. is determined by multiplying by 100, the sum of the division of

   (a) Chronological age by mental age

   (b) Chronological age by 100

   (c) Mental age by chronological age

   (d) Mental age by 100

25. **45% of the people in North India have the blood group**

(a) A

(b) B

(c) AB

(d) O

26. **When parents are of A and B blood groups the offspring will be**

(a) A group

(b) B group

(c) AB group

(d) Any of the four groups

26. **The blood group that is influenced by a recessive genes is**

(a) A

(b) B

(c) AB

(d) O

Answer sheet is at the end of the book.

Chapter 1.

EVOLUTION

1.	**(b)**	2.	**(a)**	3.	**(b)**	4.	**(c)**	5.	**(d)**
6.	**(a)**	7.	**(b)**	8.	**(b)**	9.	**(c)**	10.	**(d)**
11.	**(b)**	12.	**(a)**	13.	**(d)**	14.	**(b)**	15.	**(d)**
16.	**(d)**	17.	**(a)**	18.	**(b)**	19.	**(a)**	20.	**(c)**
21.	**(c)**	22.	**(a)**	23.	**(a)**	24.	**(b)**	25.	**(c)**
26.	**(c)**	27.	**(a)**	28.	**(b)**	29.	**(d)**	30.	**(c)**
31.	**(b)**	32.	**(a)**	33.	**(c)**	34.	**(d)**	35.	**(c)**
36.	**(d)**	37.	**(a)**	38.	**(a)**	39.	**(d)**	40.	**(b)**
41.	**(c)**	42.	**(d)**	43.	**(a)**	44.	**(b)**	45.	**(d)**
46.	**(b)**	47.	**(a)**	48.	**(b)**	49.	**(a)**	50.	**(b)**
51.	**(c)**	52.	**(d)**	53.	**(b)**	54.	**(b)**	55.	**(d)**
56.	**(c)**	57.	**(c)**	58.	**(a)**	59.	**(b)**	60.	**(d)**
61.	**(c)**	62.	**(b)**	63.	**(b)**	64.	**(c)**	65.	**(a)**
66.	**(b)**	67.	**(b)**	68.	**(b)**	69.	**(d)**	70.	**(c)**

Chapter 2.

CELL

1.	**(d)**	2.	**(b)**	3.	**(a)**	4.	**(b)**	5.	**(c)**
6.	**(d)**	7.	**(b)**	8.	**(b)**	9.	**(d)**	10.	**(c)**
11.	**(c)**	12.	**(c)**	13.	**(a)**	14.	**(b)**	15.	**(b)**
16.	**(b)**	17.	**(d)**	18.	**(b)**	19.	**(c)**	20.	**(b)**
21.	**(b)**	22.	**(a)**	23.	**(c)**	24.	**(c)**	25.	**(a)**
26.	**(c)**	27.	**(c)**	28.	**(c)**	29.	**(b)**	30.	**(d)**
31.	**(c)**	32.	**(d)**	33.	**(a)**	34.	**(c)**	35.	**(b)**
36.	**(a)**	37.	**(c)**	38.	**(c)**	39.	**(c)**	40.	**(d)**
41.	**(a)**	42.	**(a)**	43.	**(b)**	44.	**(a)**	45.	**(b)**
46.	**(a)**	47.	**(a)**	48.	**(d)**	49.	**(b)**	50.	**(d)**

51.	(d)	52.	(b)	53.	(a)	54.	(a)	55.	(b)
56.	(c)	57.	(c)	58.	(b)	59.	(b)	60.	(c)
61.	(c)	62.	(b)	63.	(c)	64.	(d)	65.	(c)
66.	(c)	67.	(b)	68.	(a)	69.	(b)	70.	(d)
71.	(b)	72.	(c)	73.	(c)	74.	(a)	75.	(d)

Chapter 3.

HISTOLOGY

1.	(c)	2.	(c)	3.	(a)	4.	(d)	5.	(a)
6.	(d)	7.	(a)	8.	(c)	9.	(c)	10.	(d)
11.	(b)	12.	(b)	13.	(b)	14.	(a)	15.	(d)
16.	(b)	17.	(c)	18.	(a)	19.	(c)	20.	(c)
21.	(a)	22.	(c)	23.	(b)	24.	(a)	25.	(b)
26.	(b)	27.	(b)	28.	(a)	29.	(c)	30.	(b)
31.	(d)	32.	(a)	33.	(a)	34.	(b)	35.	(c)
36.	(a)	37.	(c)	38.	(b)	39.	(a)	40.	(a)
41.	(c)	42.	(b)	43.	(c)	44.	(a)	45.	(c)

Chapter 4.

GENERAL PHYSIOLOGY

1.	(a)	2.	(c)	3.	(a)	4.	(d)	5.	(b)
6.	(c)	7.	(c)	8.	(b)	9.	(a)	10.	(d)
11.	(b)	12.	(b)	13.	(d)	14.	(c)	15.	(b)
16.	(a)	17.	(b)	18.	(a)	19.	(b)	20.	(d)
21.	(d)	22.	(b)	23.	(b)	24.	(b)	25.	(c)
26.	(c)	27.	(c)	28.	(c)	29.	(c)	30.	(b)
31.	( )	32.	(b)	33.	(a)	34.	( )	35.	(b)
36.	(c)	37.	(c)	38.	(d)	39.	(d)		

Chapter 5.

BLOOD AND HAEMOGLOBIN

1.	(d)	2.	(c)	3.	(a)	4.	(a)	5.	(b)
6.	(d)	7.	(d)	8.	(b)	9.	(a)	10.	(d)
11.	(b)	12.	(b)	13.	(c)	14.	(d)	15.	(c)
16.	(a)	17.	(b)	18.	(d)	19.	(d)	20.	(d)
21.	(d)	22.	(c)	23.	(a)	24.	(d)	25.	(b)
26.	(a)	27.	(c)	28.	(d)	29.	(d)	30.	(d)
31.	(c)	32.	(a)	33.	(a)	34.	(c)	35.	(b)
36.	(d)	37.	(d)	38.	(a)	39.	(d)	40.	(d)
41.	(d)	42.	(c)	43.	(c)	44.	(b)	45.	(c)
46.	(b)	47.	(d)	48.	(b)	49.	(a)	50.	(d)
51.	(c)	52.	(b)	53.	(d)	54.	(c)	55.	(a)
56.	(c)	57.	(b)						

Chapter 6.

CIRCULATORY SYSTEM

1.	(d)	2.	(a)	3.	(a)	4.	(c)	5.	(c)
6.	(b)	7.	(d)	8.	(c)	9.	(d)	10.	(c)
11.	(a)	12.	(d)	13.	(d)	14.	(a)	15.	(b)
16.	(d)	17.	(a)	18.	(c)	19.	(d)	20.	(c)
21.	(c)	22.	(c)	23.	(a)	24.	(a)	25.	(d)
26.	(d)	27.	(c)	28.	(b)	29.	(d)	30.	(d)
31.	(b)	32.	(b)	33.	(d)	34.	(b)	35.	(b)
36.	(b)	37.	(c)	38.	(b)	39.	(b)	40.	(b)
41.	(b)	42.	(c)	43.	(b)	44.	(a)	45.	(d)
46.	(b)	47.	(c)	48.	(a)	49.	(c)	50.	(d)
51.	(a)	52.	(b)	53.	(c)	54.	(b)	55.	(b)
56.	(d)	57.	(a)	58.	(c)	59.	(a)	60.	(c)
61.	(b)	62.	(b)	63.	(a)	64.	(c)	65.	(b)
66.	(b)	67.	(b)	68.	(a)	69.	(a)	70.	(b)
71.	(b)	72.	(a)	73.	(a)	74.	(a)	75.	(b)
76.	(a)								

Chapter 7.

DIGESTIVE SYSTEM

1.	(b)	2.	(c)	3.	(c)	4.	(b)	5.	(d)
6.	(a)	7.	(a)	8.	(c)	9.	(c)	10.	(a)
11.	(a)	12.	(c)	13.	(d)	14.	(b)	15.	(a)
16.	(b)	17.	(d)	18.	(c)	19.	(d)	20.	(b)
21.	(d)	22.	(b)	23.	(a)	24.	(b)	25.	(a)
26.	(c)	27.	(b)	28.	(d)	29.	(d)	30.	(c)
31.	(d)	32.	(a)	33.	(c)	34.	(d)	35.	(d)
36.	(d)	37.	(c)	38.	(d)	39.	(a)	40.	(c)
41.	(b)	42.	(c)	43.	(b)	44.	(d)	45.	(c)
46.	(d)	47.	(d)	48.	(d)	49.	(a)	50.	(d)
51.	(a)	52.	(d)	53.	(a)	54.	(a)	55.	(b)
56.	(a)	57.	(d)	58.	(c)	59.	(b)	60.	(c)
61.	(b)	62.	(a)	63.	(d)	64.	(a)	65.	(c)
66.	(a)	67.	(d)	68.	(b)	69.	(b)	70.	(c)
71.	(d)	72.	(a)	73.	(c)	74.	(a)	75.	(b)
76.	(b)	77.	(d)	78.	(d)	79.	(d)	80.	(d)
81.	(d)	82.	(c)	83.	(d)	84.	(a)	85.	(c)
86.	(c)	87.	(a)	88.	(b)	89.	(c)	90.	(b)
91.	(a)	92.	(c)	93.	(a)	94.	(a)	95.	(c)
96.	(c)	97.	(b)	98.	(a)	99.	(d)		

Chapter 8.

VITAMINS

1.	(c)	2.	(c)	3.	(b)	4.	(b)	5.	(c)
6.	(b)	7.	(d)	8.	(b)	9.	(a)	10.	(d)
11.	(b)	12.	(c)	13.	(d)	14.	(d)	15.	(a)
16.	(c)	17.	(c)	18.	(c)	19.	(d)	20.	(c)
21.	(b)	22.	(c)	23.	(d)	24.	(d)	25.	(c)

26.	**(b)**	27.	**(a)**	28.	**(b)**	29.	**(b)**	30.	**(c)**
31.	**(d)**	32.	**(d)**	33.	**(d)**	34.	**(a)**	35.	**(b)**
36.	**(c)**	37.	**(a)**	38.	**(b)**	39.	**(d)**	40.	**(d)**
41.	**(a)**	42.	**(c)**	43.	**(c)**	44.	**(d)**	45.	**(d)**
46.	**(a)**	47.	**(b)**	48.	**(b)**	49.	**(c)**	50.	**(d)**
51.	**(d)**	52.	**(d)**	53.	**(a)**				

Chapter 9.

EXCRETORY SYSTEM

1.	**(a)**	2.	**(c)**	3.	**(a)**	4.	**(c)**	5.	**(b)**
6.	**(a)**	7.	**(b)**	8.	**(c)**	9.	**(d)**	10.	**(b)**
11.	**(d)**	12.	**(a)**	13.	**(c)**	14.	**(d)**	15.	**(a)**
16.	**(d)**	17.	**(b)**	18.	**(d)**	19.	**(c)**	20.	**(a)**
21.	**(b)**	22.	**(d)**	23.	**(b)**	24.	**(c)**	25.	**(d)**
26.	**(a)**	27.	**(c)**	28.	**(b)**	29.	**(a)**	30.	**(d)**
31.	**(c)**	32.	**(b)**	33.	**(c)**	34.	**(a)**	35.	**(b)**
36.	**(c)**	37.	**(b)**	38.	**(b)**	39.	**(d)**	40.	**(b)**
41.	**(b)**	42.	**(d)**	43.	**(b)**	44.	**(d)**	45.	**(c)**
46.	**(b)**	47.	**(b)**	48.	**(b)**	49.	**(d)**	50.	**(b)**
51.	**(a)**	52.	**(c)**	53.	**(a)**	54.	**(c)**	55.	**(d)**
56.	**(c)**	57.	**(c)**	58.	**(d)**				

Chapter 10.

RESPIRATORY SYSTEM

1.	**(b)**	2.	**(d)**	3.	**(a)**	4.	**(c)**	5.	**(c)**
6.	**(a)**	7.	**(c)**	8.	**(d)**	9.	**(d)**	10.	**(c)**
11.	**(b)**	12.	**(d)**	13.	**(d)**	14.	**(d)**	15.	**(d)**
16.	**(a)**	17.	**(a)**	18.	**(a)**	19.	**(a)**	20.	**(d)**
21.	**(d)**	22.	**(c)**	23.	**(d)**	24.	**(d)**	25.	**(b)**
26.	**(d)**	27.	**(b)**	28.	**(a)**	29.	**(b)**	30.	**(d)**

31.	(b)	32.	(b)	33.	(b)	34.	(b)	35.	(a)
36.	(c)	37.	(b)	38.	(b)	39.	(c)	40.	(c)
41.	(d)	42.	(d)	43.	(b)	44.	(d)	45.	(a)
46.	(d)	47.	(d)	48.	(d)	49.	(d)	50.	(a)
51.	(d)								

Chapter 11.

HORMONES

1.	(c)	2.	(c)	3.	(b)	4.	(c)	5.	(a)
6.	(c)	7.	(d)	8.	(d)	9.	(b)	10.	(c)
11.	(d)	12.	(a)	13.	(a)	14.	(d)	15.	(d)
16.	(b)	17.	(c)	18.	(c)	19.	(a)	20.	(d)
21.	(a)	22.	(b)	23.	(d)	24.	(d)	25.	(c)
26.	(d)	27.	(d)	28.	(b)	29.	(b)	30.	(c)
31.	(a)	32.	(d)	33.	(b)	34.	(d)		

Chapter 12.

ENDOCRINE SYSTEM

1.	(d)	2.	(d)	3.	(d)	4.	(d)	5.	(a)
6.	(c)	7.	(c)	8.	(d)	9.	(d)	10.	(c)
11.	(a)	12.	(a)	13.	(b)	14.	(c)	15.	(a)
16.	(c)	17.	(d)	18.	(b)	19.	(c)	20.	(b)
21.	(d)	22.	(b)	23.	(c)	24.	(c)	25.	(b)
26.	(d)	27.	(b)	28.	(c)	29.	(c)	30.	(d)
31.	(c)	32.	(b)	33.	(d)	34.	(c)	35.	(b)
36.	(c)	37.	(c)	38.	(b)	39.	(c)	40.	(a)
41.	(a)	42.	(c)	43.	(c)	44.	(b)	45.	(b)
46.	(d)	47.	(d)	48.	(a)	49.	(b)	50.	(a)
51.	(d)	52.	(a)	53.	(b)	54.	(d)	55.	(c)
56.	(a)	57.	(c)	58.	(c)	59.	(b)	60.	(a)

61.	(d)	62.	(c)	63.	(c)	64.	(a)	65.	(c)
66.	(a)	67.	(b)	68.	(c)	69.	(b)	70.	(d)
71.	(a)	72.	(d)	73.	(b)	74.	(d)	75.	(d)
76.	(c)	77.	(b)	78.	(c)	79.	(b)	80.	(b)
81.	(b)	82.	(a)	83.	(c)	84.	(d)	85.	(b)
86.	(a)	87.	(a)	88.	(c)	89.	(b)	90.	(c)
91.	(d)	92.	(b)	93.	(a)	94.	(a)	95.	(a)
96.	(c)	97.	(a)	98.	(d)	99.	(c)	100.	(b)
101.	(c)	102.	(a)	103.	(c)	104.	(c)	105.	(b)
106.	(d)	107.	(d)	108.	(b)	109.	(a)	110.	(a)
111.	(d)	112.	(a)	113.	(a)						

Chapter 13.

REPRODUCTIVE SYSTEM

1.	(b)	2.	(d)	3.	(a)	4.	(c)	5.	(b)
6.	(b)	7.	(a)	8.	(c)	9.	(a)	10.	(a)
11.	(d)	12.	(a)	13.	(d)	14.	(d)	15.	(c)
16.	(d)	17.	(a)	18.	(b)	19.	(b)	20.	(a)
21.	(c)	22.	(b)	23.	(d)	24.	(d)	25.	(d)
26.	(d)	27.	(d)	28.	(d)	29.	(a)	30.	(d)
31.	(d)	32.	(d)	33.	(c)	34.	(d)	35.	(a)
36.	(d)	37.	(c)	38.	(d)	39.	(d)	40.	(d)
41.	(d)	42.	(d)	43.	(c)	44.	(d)	45.	(d)
46.	(b)	47.	(c)	48.	(b)	49.	(d)	50.	(d)
51.	(b)	52.	(a)	53.	(d)	54.	(d)	55.	(b)
56.	(d)	57.	(d)	58.	(c)	59.	(a)	60.	(d)
61.	(c)	62.	(d)	63.	(b)	64.	(b)	65.	(d)
66.	(d)	67.	(b)	68.	(b)	69.	(c)	70.	(a)
71.	(a)								

Chapter 14.

NERVOUS SYSTEM

1.	(a)	2.	(c)	3.	(c)	4.	(b)	5.	(d)
6.	(a)	7.	(d)	8.	(a)	9.	(b)	10.	(c)
11.	(a)	12.	(d)	13.	(b)	14.	(b)	15.	(d)
16.	(a)	17.	(b)	18.	(d)	19.	(c)	20.	(b)
21.	(c)	22.	(a)	23.	(c)	24.	(b)	25.	(c)
26.	(c)	27.	(d)	28.	(a)	29.	(b)	30.	(a)
31.	(c)	32.	(b)	33.	(a)	34.	(d)	35.	(d)
36.	(c)	37.	(c)	38.	(a)	39.	(b)	40.	(b)
41.	(d)	42.	(c)	43.	(a)	44.	(c)	45.	(a)
46.	(b)	47.	(b)	48.	(a)	49.	(a)	50.	(b)
51.	(c)	52.	(d)	53.	(c)	54.	(b)	55.	(c)
56.	(d)	57.	(a)	58.	(a)	59.	(c)	60.	(a)
61.	(a)	62.	(c)	63.	(d)	64.	(a)	65.	(d)
66.	(a)	67.	(a)	68.	(b)	69.	(c)	70.	(a)
71.	(d)	72.	(a)	73.	(b)	74.	(b)	75.	(c)
76.	(c)	77.	(d)	78.	(b)	79.	(c)	80.	(b)
81.	(d)	82.	(b)	83.	(a)	84.	(b)	85.	(c)
86.	(d)	87.	(b)	88.	(b)	89.	(c)	90.	(d)
91.	(c)	92.	(b)	93.	(d)	94.	(b)	95.	(a)
96.	(d)	97.	(d)	98.	(b)	99.	(b)	100.	(c)
101.	(c)	102.	(b)	103.	(d)	104.	(b)	105.	(d)
106.	(a)	107.	(a)	108.	(d)	109.	(a)	110.	(c)
111.	(a)	112.	(c)	113.	(c)	114.	(c)	115.	(d)
116.	(c)	117.	(b)	118.	(a)	119.	(c)	120.	(b)
121.	(b)	122.	(b)						

Chapter 15.

SPECIAL SENSES

1.	(c)	2.	(d)	3.	(a)	4.	(c)	5.	(b)
6.	(d)	7.	(b)	8.	(a)	9.	(a)	10.	(d)
11.	(c)	12.	(c)	13.	(a)	14.	(c)	15.	(d)
16.	(a)	17.	(d)	18.	(c)	19.	(b)	20.	(a)
21.	(d)	22.	(c)	23.	(c)	24.	(a)	25.	(a)
26.	(a)	27.	(b)	28.	(c)	29.	(c)	30.	(d)
31.	(c)	32.	(c)	33.	(c)	34.	(d)	35.	(c)
36.	(c)	37.	(b)	38.	(d)	39.	(b)	40.	(a)
41.	(a)	42.	(a)	43.	(c)	44.	(c)	45.	(d)
46.	(b)	47.	(a)	48.	(b)	49.	(c)	50.	(a)
51.	(c)	52.	(b)	53.	(d)	54.	(a)	55.	(a)
56.	(a)	57.	(b)						

Chapter 16.

GENETICS

1.	(b)	2.	(c)	3.	(a)	4.	(c)	5.	(b)
6.	(c)	7.	(d)	8.	(b)	9.	(a)	10.	(c)
11.	(c)	12.	(d)	13.	(b)	14.	(a)	15.	(c)
16.	(c)	17.	(a)	18.	(b)	19.	(a)	20.	(b)
21.	(a)	22.	(a)	23.	(b)	24.	(c)	25.	(b)
26.	(d)	27.	(d)						

A wide variety of Books on the following subjects by Indian and Foreign Authors are also available with us:

- Acupressure and Reflexology
- Acupuncture
- Aroma Therapy
- Astrology and Palmistry
- Ayurveda and Herbal Medicine
- Bach Flower Remedies
- Biochemistry
- Crystal and Gem Therapy
- Dowsing - Pendulam
- Feng Shui
- Health Care
- Holistic Medicine
- Homoeopathy

- Hypnosis
- Iridology
- Juice and Food Therapy
- Magnetotherapy
- Medical Dictionary
- Nature Cure
- Pet Animals
- Pranic Healing
- Reiki and Spiritualism
- Tai Chi
- Tarot
- Urine Therapy
- Vaastu
- Yoga

A detailed catalogue of books is available with B. Jain Publishers (P) Ltd. on request.

Acupressure, Magnetic and Feng Shui gadgets are also available.

SUBSCRIPTION COUPON

Yes, I want to subscribe to The Homoeopathic Heritage.

SUBSCRIPTION RATES FOR ONE YEAR

OVERSEAS CUSTOMERS

BANGLADESH	PAKISTAN	REST OF THE WORLD
$ 18/-	$ 32/-	$ 40/-

INDIAN CUSTOMERS

INDIA	NEPAL	BHUTAN
Rs. 200/-	Rs. 200/-	Rs. 200/-

MODE OF PAYMENT

For India, Nepal & Bhutan by M.O., Bank Draft or Cheque payable at Delhi, New Delhi in favour of **B. Jain Publishers (P) Ltd.,** 1921/10, Chuna Mandi, Paharganj, Post Box 5775, New Delhi-55, India.

For Overseas by International Money Order or Bank Draft in favour of **B. Jain Publishers Overseas,** 1920, Street No. 10th, Chuna Mandi, Post Box 5775, Paharganj, New Delhi - 110 055, India.

SUBSCRIPTION ORDER FORM
(Write in Capitals)

Name ....

Complete Mailing Address ....

....

....

.... Pin ....

Ph. (Res.) .... Ph. (Off.) ....

E-mail ....

I am remitting Rs./US$ .... by M.O./Bank Draft/Cheque

Date ....   Signature